RICHARD SIMMONS'
NEVER GIVE UP

RICHARD SIMMONS'
NEVER GIVE UP

INSPIRATIONS, REFLECTIONS, STORIES OF HOPE

♦

RICHARD SIMMONS

WARNER BOOKS

A Time Warner Company

Grateful acknowledgment is given to Winifred Morice for her poetry on pages 45, 69, 144-145, 197-198, 259-260, and 313.

Photographs on page 310 reprinted by permission of the *Portsmouth Daily News*.

Warner Books, Inc., 1271 Avenue of the Americas, New York, NY 10020

W A Time Warner Company

Printed in the United States of America
First Printing: February 1993
10 9 8 7 6 5 4 3 2

Library of Congress Cataloging-in-Publication Data

Simmons, Richard.
    [Never give up]
    Richard Simmons' never give up : inspirations, reflections, stories of hope / Richard Simmons.
        p.   cm.
    ISBN 0-446-51703-8
    1. Reducing.   2. Affirmations.   I. Title.
RM222.2.S545   1993
613.2'5—dc20
                                            92-50139
                                              CIP

Book design by Giorgetta Bell McRee

ACKNOWLEDGMENTS

"Elijah, I know you have worked with me for ten years now . . . and I know you have helped me on a lot of projects, but I really need your assistance with my next exciting project!"

"What project are you talking about?"

"I'm writing a new book and I want you to help me."

Elijah's eyes grew very big as he gasped: "A book . . . I've never worked on a book before! I can't do that!"

"Oh yes you can," I answered. "How many letters have we outlined together? Thousands! Who was the editor of my newsletter for five years? You Elijah. Admit it . . . you're a writer! So come on . . . are you with me?"

Elijah smiled and said, "I'd be honored to be part of your book, Richard."

And the next day we began writing.

You see Elijah, I told you we could do it. Thank you Elijah for giving up your Saturdays and Sundays. Thank you for skipping a well-deserved vacation and canceling your trip back home to Mississippi to see your mama. Thank you for putting your heart and soul on to these pages.

Elijah Jones, I love you and respect you very much.

CONTENTS

NEVER GIVE UP

vii   RICHARD SIMMONS'

FOREWORD

"Good afternoon . . . may I speak with Helen Lambert?"

". . . and who's this?"

"It's Richard Simmons calling."

"Sure . . . and I'm Mother Teresa!" (Click!)

This is not the first time someone has accused me of "not being Richard Simmons." In my line of work you get used to it.

I redial the number . . . it's ringing. . . .

"Yeah, and who are you now?"

"Doug, please don't hang up the phone again."

I found myself talking a little faster, "I am really Richard Simmons and I'm calling because your wife wrote me . . ."

"Hey . . . how did you know my name was Doug?"

"Because, like I said, your wife, Helen, wrote me a long letter about her weight and she told me all about you!"

"What did she say about me?"

"Doug, this stuff is personal. Please let me talk to Helen!"

"She's . . . she's not here. She went to pick up the pizza. Oh my God . . . I shouldn't have told you that! Hey Rich, please don't mention the pizza thing please, she'll kill me!"

"What kind of pizza?"

"This stuff is personal . . . if I can't ask you what Helen said about me, you can't ask any pizza questions!"

"That's fair. I'll call back in an hour. Bye, Doug."

"Wanna come over for a slice? . . . Just kidding . . . bye!"

I waited an hour and dialed the Lambert number. Doug answered the phone again. He pretended to be surprised and I played along with him.

"Honey, you're never going to believe who's on the phone! It's Richard Simmons!" His "performance" deserved an Oscar!

Helen and I talked for a while. She was a little down about her weight and I tried my best to cheer her up. I managed to have her laughing by the end of the conversation. That's always one of my goals. I call myself the "phone clown." Making people laugh and feel better about themselves is my specialty and I practice every day.

There are times I feel possessed by the Chatty Kathy doll because I spend so many hours on the phone with people I have never met. Many of you know that I do this. While you are reading this book you may be chuckling to yourself about the time I called *you.*

This all started back in the late 70s when I got the opportunity to spread my lo-cal message on the very popular soap opera, "General Hospital." The effect of each letter's story was overwhelming and whenever one of them tugged particularly at my heart, I would be moved to pick up the phone and talk to the other person. Fourteen years later it's the same: people keep writing and I keep calling.

Why? There are two important reasons. Reason Number One, I know that the growing overweight and out of shape population needs constant encouragement. Reason Number Two, this daily interaction

RICHARD SIMMONS'

NEVER GIVE UP

with you helps me continue my lifelong crusade. It's "practice what you preach." For me, that also means . . . "*eat* what you *preach*."

When I tell others to hang in there and take care of their health, I am talking to myself as well. You see, after all these caloric counting years, I still struggle with food. You'd think it would be easy for me by now, but it's not and it never will be.

What keeps me up, energized and motivated? Well, it's stories like the ones you are about to read. These are all "real people," their stories come directly from their letters. I've hopped on hundreds of airplanes and driven thousands of miles to meet many of them personally. I must tell you, the hardest part of writing this book was when I would call each person to read the story back. Inevitably, the reaction of the person on the other end of the phone would be so strong I could relive their sad times over with them in that moment. It's one thing to live it and another to have someone read it back to you.

So with their permission, I have put together this collection of short stories for those who are still struggling with something in their lives. Each of the unique people in this book will give you the courage and strength to keep fighting. You may relive some painful moments of your own. I did. You may even find some answers to questions you've been asking yourself for years. One thing is for sure though, you will be inspired.

Each story will take you five or ten minutes to read. That's about the same amount of time it would take you to finish a few slices of pizza. So when the urge hits you, spend a few inspirational moments with some of the people gathered together here. Follow these personal journeys and *Never Give Up*.

RICHARD SIMMONS

GUINEA PIG

Richard's Story

*M*ilton would try anything to lose weight. Just ten-years-old and already he was tired of the name calling and put-downs that were part of his daily existence. Milton took suggestions from everyone in the neighborhood. Frankie, who owned the corner grocery store, swore that cottage cheese was the "only way to diet."

"White erasers in a creamy sauce, yeech! It doesn't sound too thrilling to me, Mr. Raffino, but I'll try it," Milton said. So he bought his first carton and took it home. Milton tried at least three times to like the cottage cheese but no matter how he doctored it up, it was still "white erasers in a milky sauce." A Milky Way was the only way to get that diet taste out of his mouth.

Ella, the lady across the street, read all the latest movie magazines. She insisted tuna would be Milton's best friend. When he opened that little round can and got his first whiff of that special Chicken of the Sea fragrance, well, Milton decided he didn't want a best friend that smelled like cat food!

For a while there in high school Milton tried counting calories. The whole day was spent adding up all the calories in the food he was eating. "Well, it's a small apple . . . plus I'm not eating the stem or the core and I'm certainly not eating the skin so this apple should only cost me forty-three calories," he said. "And this chocolate turtle looks so small to me and one of the big nuts is missing so I can deduct twenty-eight calories from that!" Milton nearly drove himself nuts, besides, he always did hate math, so the counting stopped.

While the counting may have stopped, the diets never did. Milton stayed on the grapefruit, hard boiled egg and melba toast diet for eight hours . . . the rice diet for two days and the eat-all-you-want-of-one-food diet lasted five days. That was a record for Milton. Five days on a single diet was about all he could muster the willpower for.

By the time Milton was in college he had gotten his own subscription to *Cosmopolitan*, a magazine that offered a different diet every month. And every month Milton tried that latest diet, lasting on it for less than a week. One of the guys in Milton's class stole a few diet pills from his sister's prescription bottle and gave them to Milton to try. But Milton had just finished reading his mother's copy of Jacqueline Susann's *Valley of the Dolls* and decided "pills were ill."

Liquid diets were getting a lot of play in the news and Milton was first in line to experiment once again. "This is so easy. No cooking, no pots or pans to clean up, no more grocery shopping, just these chocolate malts five times a day. I can do that!" He bought the packets of powder, a new blender and started to drink his fat away. Why, it was a miracle! Three days passed, and Milton was still drinking meals through a straw. A week passed, then twenty-eight days and Milton had lost forty-one pounds. Thinking that he was out of the diet woods, Milton began exchanging one of the malts for a pizza or a plate of barbecue spareribs. Milton began to eat again. Twenty-eight days without food, he thought. This is not natural. The packets of diet powder were banned to the cupboard, the blender was cleaned out and put away and the forty-one pounds came back on in all the same places.

"What's that in your ear?" Milton asked his friend, Susie.

"Oh, it's a staple," she said. "The doctor put it in my ear to help me lose weight. When I start to feel hungry I just thump my ear like this," she said, giving her ear a little thump, "and the desire for food goes away." Well, it all sounded very promising to Milton, but as they were talking about the new weight loss method, Susie was finishing up the last couple bites of an ice-cream sandwich. Milton didn't have the nerve to tell her that he thought it might be a good time to give that ear a couple more thumps!

Milton skipped the ear staple and decided that fasting was going to be the way he would get rid of the fat forever. For two and a half months Milton ate no food and drank only water. One hundred and twenty three pounds later, Milton was thin. He was sick, but he was thin. He had starved himself all the way down to 119 pounds. He could actually count his ribs. Milton came close to losing his life—came close to dying

3   RICHARD SIMMONS'

NEVER GIVE UP

because of dieting. If this story is starting to sound familiar to you, well, it's because this is my story. My real name is Milton, not Richard, and that's the life I lived. I thought since I was writing a storybook, I would start by telling you my own story. I wanted you to read what I went through and what I learned. The magic word here is *learned*. With all the diets I have been on in my lifetime, I truly learned nothing. Diets aren't driven by education but by panic. I stopped panicking and started to put together a formula that would work for me and my eating habits. I wanted a plan that was liveable—one that would eliminate feelings of guilt and punishment. I approached and welcomed these changes but at the same time I wanted to do this slowly and not run a race with myself. I came to grips with the fact that I was a compulsive eater and I was going to be a compulsive eater until God stopped my chewing.

I had tried hating the food, I had tried quitting the food, now I had to simply *get along* with the food. With that acceptance, I started to assemble my program.

I was in my office cleaning out a bookshelf and I came upon a little, dark green book someone had given me for Christmas a few years ago. It was a children's textbook called *Health for Today*. I looked at the copyright and was surprised to see that the book was written for the public school system in 1948, the year I was born. The first chapter was about the basic food groups—bread, dairy, meat, fruit, vegetables and fat. "Oh, I know this stuff," I said to myself, but did I really? The book stated "the balance of correct portions of all the food groups is the secret to health." Balance and portions—that's the secret! That's all I needed to hear. I knew after twenty years of dieting that any program under 1,000 calories was not playing it safe and I could possibly get sick. I was going to train myself to plot out this 1,000 Live-It program instead of "diet" program.

I paid a visit to the neighborhood art store and bought construction paper in all the colors of the six food groups. I cut the sheets up in squares the size of playing cards. I figured out grams of protein, carbohydrates and fat and figured out all the calories for all the groups. I got out my measuring cup and spoons and went to work dividing up the foods that I could have every day. I listed on the colored pieces of paper what each card could buy, for instance, one fruit card would allow you a half cup of grapefruit juice or twelve grapes, one fat card listed choices like one teaspoon of butter, one tablespoon of salad dressing or six nuts. I then constructed a wallet out of plastic that would hold the cards for 1,000 calories. Two fruit cards, three bread, two vegetable, two dairy, three meat and three fat cards. I had a few calories left over so I created joker cards—fatless snack cards that could buy you one sugarfree fruit juice bar or a dill pickle, just as long as it was under thirty-five calories. That added up to 1,000 calories and now I was all ready to start pulling my cards.

It became my personal food calculator. When I ate breakfast I would move the appropriate cards to the slot on the other side of the wallet. I'd eat a half cup of cereal, a cup of nonfat milk and an orange. I'd move over one bread, one dairy and one fruit card. By moving the cards I was taking the responsibility of eating that meal and seeing exactly what I had left over for the rest of the day. I was planning my meals instead of pouting about them. When I moved all the cards over and there weren't any food cards left for me to pick, I knew I had eaten the right amount of everything and I had stayed true-blue to the 1,000 calories. I did not feel abandoned and I actually wasn't hungry for more.

I remember going to bed after pulling those cards for the first day. I remember having a good feeling because I had succeeded. I slept well knowing I had already started tomorrow on a positive note. When I completed one week on 1,000 calories, I adjusted my cards up to 1,200 calories a day and stayed on that for a week.

Now I know I didn't discover electricity or a fancy computer that helps man orbit in space, but I have put together a system that finally taught me how to eat and I was very proud of it. I showed it to doctors, dieticians and nutritionists, then fine-tuned my plastic wallet and cards. I called my plan Deal-A-Meal.

In order to stay on Deal-A-Meal I needed to stay motivated—my biggest problem—yours, too, huh! I began thinking of ways to keep myself jazzed and positive. Since compliments are the highest form of flattery I started letting myself know that I was a pretty terrific person. I got up in the morning, looked in the mirror and said "I am worth it!" After a few weeks of talking in the mirror I started to believe I *was* worth it. I added another line to my new ritual, "I am going all the way." Over a period of time I collected twenty-one of these thoughts. I wrote them down on a sheet of paper and taped it to the bathroom mirror. Instead of tearing myself down and being negative I would simply take the time to build myself up so I'd be strong and most important, I'd keep trying. I called these twenty-one thoughts my "Project Me Passport."

I was now armed with a solid knowledge about food and a stronger will to help my insides. Now I had to do something about my outside—the body that I had neglected for so long. Being the fat kid I never, without exception, played sports and I never saw my own sweat. Exercise to me was the strength required to open a stubborn bag of Chips Ahoys! I swallowed hard and went out looking for a gym or health club where I would feel comfortable.

Since this "exercise thing" was so new to me, I started taking different classes around town, searching for the perfect class for me. I always felt like the ugly duckling. Everyone looked so perfect, so thin. I knew I was standing out like a chubby thumb. For two years, I gym and club hopped trying weights, machines, swimming and yoga. Frankly it was all just too serious for me. I wanted to have fun! I thought, Hey, if you had so much fun putting that weight on, you should have some fun taking it off, too!

I went home, got out some of my favorite records and started creating my very own exercise class. For an hour or so a day I could warm up my body, take a combination of dance movements—like the grapevine, the pony and the twist—and go to town. I'd raise my arms and shake them, I'd kick my legs and sing along to all the tunes. Something unbelievable happened—I began to sweat!

It took awhile but I finally mastered my new healthy life-style. I knew there would be a lot of people who could benefit from this plan I'd put together. I knew I could teach them an eating program they could live with, a few mental tricks for their attitude and a safe exercise class they'd go nuts over. I opened Slimmons in Beverly Hills and I was right. They came, they laughed and they lost.

RICHARD SIMMONS'

NEVER GIVE UP

I have been teaching and working this program for over a decade and a half. It has not been easy for me and I have to admit, there have been times when Milton has slipped back into my life. But I'd only let him in for one meal and then I would go back to the three tools that always pulled me through. I'd go back to the sentences taped on my mirror, I'd try my best to control the food and I never missed exercise. It was my life insurance, my guarantee that I would be burning some calories that day.

This way of life, and believe me, it is a way of life, well, it's timeless. There will never be an easier or quicker way to achieve good health. Please learn from my story and don't *you* fall for anything and everything that comes along like I did. Look at it this way, I've been your guinea pig. I've done your lab work, I've been obese, I've been bone thin. I've settled on a weight of 150 pounds (plus a five-pound cushion— thank God for that cushion). One hundred nineteen pounds was too low. I had to starve to stay at 138 pounds so at 150 I feel "just right." I have to eat 1,800 calories, 20 grams of fat a day plus exercise an hour to maintain those numbers on the scale. I just want to know who invented that darn scale anyway. I'm sure it was some thin person who could eat all day long and never gain an ounce . . . in my next life!

Well, that's my story and the philosophy I live by. I hope it helps. Oh, I just wanted you to know, I ended up loving cottage cheese and have devoured thousands of cans of water packed tuna and yes, I still get *Cosmo* and look at the monthly diet. Milton still lives here.

I admit I love food and I am addicted to it.

◆

My weight bothers me and I know it's not healthy.

◆

I am overweight for the most part because I overeat and don't exercise enough.

◆

THE PROMISE

Tommy's Story

*I*f I had to choose one word that links all the letters I get from you together, that word would be *help*. Tommy's letter asked for help but his words seemed to be reaching for more than that. More than a plea for help, I felt that Tommy was sending out an SOS!

He told me he didn't have any idea how much he weighed; there wasn't a scale anywhere that he thought would go high enough. What he did know was that he weighed so much he had spent over a whole year living his life in a BarcaLounger recliner. He lacked the strength to get up and move around anymore, except for the shortest of distances inside his home. I could picture him in my mind living that way, he deserved better, all of us deserve better. I was going to do my best to throw Tommy a lifeline!

When I called him, his wife answered the phone. It was obvious she was so glad that I had called. "Hold on, Richard," she said. "I know that Tommy will *really* want to talk to you." Tommy got on the line and his voice sounded very hopeless.

"Richard, I wrote you only ten days ago. I knew it was a long shot that I'd hear from you but, man, am I glad you called."

Well, I told Tommy that my getting in touch with him would never again be a long shot and I wanted to do all I could to get him out of that recliner and back on his feet.

He told me he'd always been heavy, plus he's a big guy anyway: tall. His adoration for good food followed him from childhood to adulthood but he said he never let the weight bother him. At 400 pounds he was still going to work every day until his health deteriorated to the point where he couldn't. Left with nothing to do all day but eat, he said, "I just started eating my life away." I asked him what he did all day to keep himself from getting bored.

"Oh, I'm a ham radio operator, Richard. I may not be able to go see them but I have a bunch of friends I talk to over the airwaves every day. They tell me about the latest movies, the weather, what they did over the weekend, they keep me from feeling so out of touch with the rest of the world."

Tommy also told me he had a beautiful wife, Sandra, who took good care of him and a son, Matthew, who was about to graduate from high school.

"And you know what hurts me the most right now," he said. "I'm so heavy, I won't be able to attend my son's graduation. That hurts, Richard. He's a good boy and it really hurts."

Tommy's voice changed. The sadness I'd heard

when he picked up the phone had begun to go away but returned when he began talking about his son. I told him that I was sorry he wouldn't be able to make Matthew's graduation and I wanted to do a little something to cheer him up.

"I'm going to send you my Deal-A-Meal program, Tommy. Now, like I told you, I do want to help, but there is something very important I want you to keep in the back of your mind—you have to want to help yourself. I wish there were a magic wand I could just wave to make those pounds go away but the honest truth is, *you* are going to have to do this . . . and you know what, Tommy, . . . you can."

He thanked me again for calling and said he would be looking for my package. He told me, "When it comes, Richard, I promise you I'll use it, I promise you I'm going to try and lose this weight. I really do mean that!"

"Uh-uh, Tommy," I said, "don't make that promise to me because you're promising the wrong guy. I want you to make that same promise . . . to yourself! I'll be checking with you real soon, okay?"

When his package arrived, Tommy experienced a feeling that had been missing from his life in a long time . . . hope! He told his wife, "If Richard Simmons, as busy as you figure he's gotta be, thinks enough of me to call and send me this thing—well, I'd be pretty foolish not to use it. Sandra, I'm going to try and do this. Somebody out there believes in me, maybe it's time I start believing in myself." It would be some time before Tommy confided this to me, but when he did, I was touched.

Tommy had taken that all-important first step, he had a made-up mind, he was ready to start.

Tommy became what can best be called a "food

manager"; each morning he'd take time out to plan his meals for that day. "Let's see, for breakfast, I'll have a little bowl of cereal, some low-fat milk and a piece of fruit. Lunchtime, hmm . . . a hamburger roll, one ounce sliced turkey with mustard, lettuce, tomato and mayo . . . no, wait, mayo, that's a fat, I'll save my fat card for a little dressing on my salad at dinner. Dinner! Okay, this is Thursday . . . must be pork chops. I'll have *half* a pork chop, my salad, Sandra will make a vegetable dish probably and I'll have a NutraSweet ice-cream bar for dessert. There, I've done it!"

And let me tell you, Tommy really *was* doing it. His weight was on the way down *and* now he had a way to keep track. His uncle had heard about my phone call to him and told Tommy, "Well, if you're gonna do this right, you've got to have a scale. Why don't you take my old grain scale and set it up in your basement. I'm not using it anymore!"

So Tommy did have a starting point . . . 612 pounds! That was then but this is now—he lost ninety pounds in two months. But that's only part of the story. Already, he was able to say good-bye and *gladly* to his old BarcaLounger and get out of the house. He sent me a photo of himself at his highest weight sitting outside on a special bench his father had built for him. But there was a new photo of Tommy, *standing*, not sitting in the same spot looking much smaller, healthier and happier!

I showed this picture to everyone in my office, "Just look at him," I said. "Isn't he incredible! Let's get him on the phone!"

"Tommy," I shouted into the receiver, "Tommy, I'm so glad for you. I'm sitting here looking at your picture. You must be awfully proud, how do you feel?"

Tommy told me he felt set free. He didn't have to depend on his ham radio to experience life anymore. He was out there getting a taste of it himself! He weighed himself once a week on Sunday mornings after breakfast and couldn't believe how much weight he was losing. He told me each week's weight loss was all he needed to help inspire him for the next week and told me, "Watch your mailbox, the next photo will show me, not at five hundred but four hundred pounds!"

And sure enough, three months later, a photo of Tommy arrived.

He wasn't just weighing himself either, he weighed his foods, calculated his exchanges and kept right on going. Tommy was living like never before, his ham radio buddies became his fan club. "Tommy, how much have you lost now? What's that . . . I believe we got a little interference . . . did you say two hundred and thirty-six pounds? Man, oh man . . . you are outta sight . . . I mean, for real!"

Tommy was like a kid again! He was snowmobiling, riding all-terrain vehicles with his dad, even worked in the pit stop for a friend who was a race car driver. But Tommy's favorite form of exercise was doing something he'd been unable to do in a long time . . . walking hand in hand with his wife, Sandra!

I thought back to that lonely, melancholy voice I'd heard less than a year before and looked at what Tommy was doing today and thought: It sure would be nice to meet this amazing man. But that would have to wait. I was having an extremely busy summer traveling, teaching at my club, plus I had a brand-new show to tape.

We had flown in a group of people who'd changed their lives as Tommy had to appear with me. Those

RICHARD SIMMONS'

NEVER GIVE UP

taping days are *always* crazy. What with the cameras, the lighting, building a set . . . I'll tell you, it gets tough, even for me, to keep up.

The day went well, though. Everyone I interviewed did a great job after being a little nervous at first with all the cameras. But the day was over, it was time to wrap up and for me to go home and soak in a nice long bubble bath . . . or so I thought!

"Richard, don't leave yet, okay!" It was a voice I know very well booming across the set. It was Ed, my director and partner.

"Ed, we're done!" I whined. "You said wrap five minutes ago! Aren't we finished?"

"Well, not quite. You spend so much time surprising everyone else . . . well, this time the surprise is on you. . . . Now, sit down, face the camera and don't move!"

I didn't know what on earth was going on. I mean, you never know with Ed! I was sitting on the sofa of our living room set when this person came out from behind me and said, "Hi, Richard . . . I'm Tommy!" My staff has pulled a lot of stunts on me over the years and I'm not the easiest person to put one over on, but I've got to hand it to them, they really got me this time!

"Tommy! You're here . . . how . . . what! . . ." I got up, threw my arms around him and I'm sorry, but I did it again . . . I cried! Tommy had lost almost three hundred pounds and he might as well have been Tommy Selleck, as far as I was concerned.

After I got over the initial shock, we sat down and talked! His dream of freedom was real now, he really was a new man. Tommy asked me, "Remember how hurt I was that I missed Matthew's graduation . . . well he moved out a few weeks ago to start college and I was his moving partner. We loaded the truck together and everything and I've promised *myself* that I will attend his graduation next time, that's for sure."

"I know you will, too, Tommy," I said. "By the way, what are you doing for dinner tonight? I want you to join us at Spago's. Everybody's worked so hard, we thought it'd be a nice evening out." Tommy said he'd love to join!

You know the old saying: "Turnabout is fair play?" Well, I decided I was ready to play. Dinner was planned for 8:00 P.M. but I was going to be a little late, or at least I wanted everyone to think I was!

I drove home and changed, not into my dinner outfit, but my waiter's outfit! I put on this brown wig and tucked away every curl out of sight . . . that took some doing. I applied a mustache, a pair of wire frame glasses and voilà . . . Nick, the waiter was ready to report for duty.

I'd called ahead to the staff at Spago's and they were very helpful with my plot. I arrived at the restaurant before everyone else and as the table began to fill with "my customers," and after a while everyone was going: "Well, where's Richard?" "Sir, would you like another roll?" I asked Tommy. "Oh, no thank you, I'm fine," he replied. (I was so proud of him.) Let me tell you, I put food on the table, I directed people to the restroom, no one had any idea it was me.

"Gosh, it's almost 9:00 P.M., I hope nothing happened to Richard," someone said. I couldn't take it any longer and keep this up without blowing it anyway so . . . I reached into my pocket and started passing around the Fat Cards from one of my Deal-A-Meal Programs.

I stood there with hands folded in front of me,

trying my very best to hold back a grin as everybody tried to figure out, "What does this mean?" I couldn't stand it anymore and burst out laughing . . . talk about losing it!

Well, everybody had to admit, including Ed, my payback was pretty darn good!

After dinner, I told Tommy I would be teaching class at Slimmons the next day. Since he had a couple extra days in Los Angeles, I wanted him to be there. "Hey Tommy . . . you're moving pretty good!" I shouted to him in class. After watching his low calorie performance at Spago's and his high energy show at the club, I knew Tommy was in good shape in more ways than one!

I felt like he was doing fine on his own and needed less of my help these days. So some time passed between our L.A. meeting and our next conversation . . . too much time! When I'm at home in Los Angeles, the weekends are when I really catch up with my mail and make phone calls. I hadn't planned to call Tommy but for some reason, felt compelled to. So I did.

"Tommy, it's been awhile since we talked . . . how're you doing?"

"Well, Richard . . ." he started, and I'll tell you, the tone of his voice sounded too much like the one I'd heard a year earlier, something was wrong.

I interrupted him, "Tommy, are you okay, how are you doing?"

"Richard, my father passed away not too long ago, his death was kind of sudden and I didn't take it too well. You know, we were very close."

I thought back to when I lost my own father and I know what it's like to lose someone that special. I told Tommy how sorry I was to hear his news. I asked if there was anything I could do. He thanked me and said he would be all right, it would just take some time.

"How's your weight?" I asked. There was a pause on the line . . . "Tommy, how's your weight?"

"Not good, Richard . . . not good! Since I lost my dad I've been coping with it the best way I know how."

"You're eating again, aren't you, Tommy?" There was another pause.

"Yep . . . yep, I'm eating again."

"Tommy, your dad watched you go from being almost a total shut-in to creating a brand-new life for yourself," I said. "How would he feel to know that his death has caused you to, well . . . how else can I put it, you're killing yourself again!"

"I guess I'm pretty bad, huh, Richard?"

"Bad?" I asked. "Tommy, gaining weight doesn't make you a bad person. What you've got to do now is bring back that person we both knew just a few months ago. I guarantee you nothing would make your father happier than that! Is the scale still in the basement?"

"Yep!"

"Do you know how much you've gained?"

"Nope."

"Well, I'll hold! Go downstairs right now, get on that scale, I want to know how much you've gained."

I waited for Tommy to get downstairs and when he got back on the phone with me, he was talking from the basement telephone.

"Bad news, Richard . . . I've put on sixty-seven pounds!"

I told Tommy, "Okay, so you've put on sixty-seven pounds but it ain't over yet. You know how to do it,

19   RICHARD SIMMONS'

so let's get back on the program. It's time to make that promise all over again. And if I have to call you every day . . . I will."

Tommy told me, "I'm going to try again, Richard. I'm going to try again. You're right. I know I can do it and frankly, I miss the old me, too!"

We said good-bye and just two days later I called him right back.

"So Tommy . . . how's it going so far?"

"So far . . . so far, so good, Richard. I tell you I really do feel better already. I'm not going to weigh in until Sunday . . . just like I used to. I know it's early, it's only been two days but honestly, I feel like it's going to happen again, I really do!"

"Hang in there, Tommy. I can hear the old you coming back already. I told you once before . . . you can do this. I'll call to check up on you in a few days . . . next Sunday . . . after breakfast!"

Tommy must have been waiting by the phone when I called him on Sunday. He answered, "Hello . . . Richard?"

"Hey, I didn't even hear it ring," I said. "And how'd you know it was going to be me?"

"When you say you're gonna call, Richard . . . you always do . . . besides, I couldn't wait to tell you . . . I'm *really* doing great. I mowed my own lawn today and I mowed my mother's lawn yesterday. I haven't felt this good in a long time."

"Now that's the Tommy I know," I said, "And how about the weight, did you get on the scale this morning?"

"Yep, and I lost eleven pounds already!"

"Yahooo," I shouted! "I knew you could do it!"

"Hey, Richard . . . that's not all," he said, "My

21   RICHARD SIMMONS'

NEVER GIVE UP

mom's birthday was yesterday, we had this big cake and everything and I didn't have a bite!"

"Well, Tommy, you could have had a teeny piece, you know!"

"Nahhh, Richard, you know I really didn't want it. Hey, I gotta tell you something else I did."

"Yeah, what's that," I asked.

"Mom wanted to visit Dad at the cemetery so I drove her and I had a little chance to talk to him alone. I told him not to worry about me because I know I'm going to be all right now."

Relieved is the only way I can describe my feelings after hanging up with Tommy. He'd come to realize that the loss of his father was no reason to give up on himself, it was no reason for the world to lose Tommy. When he chose to reclaim his good health, Tommy also chose the best possible way of honoring the memory of his dad.

UNFINISHED BUSINESS

Diane's Story

*T*he greatest reward in my life is knowing that so many people have lost weight because of my program. I know that a lot of you lose the weight, gain it back and lose again: the yo-yo syndrome. You know, it's like so much "unfinished business," not good for your health, much less your attitude. I'm proud of you for trying. But you must keep trying. There's a great reward waiting for you when you reach that goal!

Then, there are those of you, and I'm also proud of this group, that lose the weight and keep it off, period! You will get your halos in heaven, surely. But as I read your mail, talk to you on the phone and meet you in person, I discover that you don't stop there. The weight loss oftentimes inspires you to change something else in your life that you've put off doing. You've lost the weight, you look good and yet in your mind, you still feel like you have "unfinished business." The story I'm about to tell you is about a woman who tied up a big loose end in her life after reaching her goal weight.

Diane was nineteen-years-old when she met the "man of her dreams." The two of them were madly, passionately in love; this was a serious relationship. When Diane discovered she was pregnant, she just knew in her heart that when she told her boyfriend they had a baby on the way, he would be thrilled and automatically suggest they get married.

But her heart was wrong. When she broke the news to him, instead of him saying, "A baby, that's wonderful, let's get married, get a home, raise a family," he told her, "Well, that's your problem. I'm not ready for a baby, a family, none of that stuff yet!" He said good-bye, good luck, and he vanished from her life.

Diane was naturally crushed, the man she loved and thought she knew was just an illusion. What was she going to do now? Still a teenager, living at home with her parents, her choices were few. It was 1966, abortion was illegal in her state and besides she wanted to have her baby anyway. Her parents were very strict and would not take the news they were going to be "unwed" grandparents very well at all. Diane didn't want to bring shame on them or herself, so she kept her pregnancy a secret from them the entire nine months. She began dressing in big blousy tops and wore lots of overcoats to hide her condition. She didn't even tell anyone on her job. Diane worked at, of all places, St. Agnes Foundling Home. It was a home for unwed mothers as well as an adoption agency! She was a secretary there to Sister Edna.

By the ninth month, of course, Diane would not

be able to keep her condition a secret any longer. She was at home with her parents and her sister when she went into labor right in the living room. The family was panicked at first until her mother figured out exactly what was "wrong" with her.

They helped her to the car and everyone, including her sister, were in the car as they rushed her to the hospital in the next county, twenty miles away. There was total silence in the car except for Diane's crying, "I'm sorry, I'm sorry."

Diane lay on a delivery table sobbing out loud as she wondered how all this would turn out. Her crying stopped when a plastic cup was placed over her nose, she was breathing ether and soon drifted into sleep.

When Diane woke up the next morning in a hospital bed, she had no idea how the previous evening had ended. She lay there as tears streamed down her face. There was no baby to hold, to cuddle or to sing to, just Diane. She was not alone for long. A social worker came into the room to have a little talk with her.

"Good morning, I hope you're not in any pain and I realize this must be difficult for you. I've talked to your parents. They feel now is not the time for you to be trying to raise a child, especially without a husband. With your okay, we're going to put the baby up for adoption, but as I said, we'll need approval from you."

Diane had a very difficult decision to make. Knowing her parents were upset enough already, she feared making a bad situation even worse. In an effort to make peace, she reluctantly agreed to give up the baby but asked, "Can I at least see her?"

"Well, of course you can. Her name is Trisha, by the way." Diane wondered how *her* baby already had

25   RICHARD SIMMONS'

NEVER GIVE UP

a name but she was beyond asking questions at this point. "Are you strong enough to walk? We can go right now."

The social worker helped Diane out of bed and walked with her to the nursery. Through a glass window, a nurse picked up one of the several new babies and held her up as Diane stared at the life she had carried inside her for nine months. For two very short minutes she looked at her daughter, Trisha, through the tears in her eyes. There was her baby, so close and yet so very far away. The social worker took her by the arm, it was time to go.

When she was allowed to go home, Diane's family didn't mistreat her or criticize her for having a child out of wedlock. She almost wished they had, though. Absolutely nothing was ever said about her baby; it's like they say, the silence was deafening. It was her parents who drove her to the courthouse where Diane made giving up her baby official. She signed a release for Trisha to be placed in the hands of a foster home. After she wrote her signature, the judge took her hand and looked her squarely in the eyes and said, "I'm sorry, you will forget."

But Diane did not forget. The emptiness she'd felt the morning after giving birth was still every bit as strong and present now. The image of her beautiful baby by now in a stranger's home haunted her for months to come.

Diane had always eaten more than she should have, but she'd never been obese. After losing her baby, however, food became more important than ever. Food became the one thing that made her feel at least a little better. She may not have had a baby to cuddle but she could cuddle herself with food.

Several months after losing the baby, Diane met a

new boyfriend. She didn't want to have any more secrets so she told him right up front about getting pregnant and giving the child up for adoption. He told her that he didn't mind, appreciated her honesty and that he still loved her.

They were married just a few months later and before they had a chance to really get used to being husband and wife, he was sent off to serve in Vietnam. When he returned stateside two years later, Diane could see that the war had changed him. They had two sons together but they fought constantly and it wasn't long before the only way to solve their problems was through a divorce.

Diane raised her two sons on her own. She continued to overeat and also almost every day, she dreamed about her first child, her daughter, and wondered where she might be.

Diane remained divorced for seven years until she fell in love again with a divorcé who had custody of his four children. Diane had told him her adoption story right up front and he also accepted her. He married Diane and their new, large family got even larger when they had two more babies together. The second time around was like magic, she had a great husband, eight lovely children and a persistent gnawing feeling in her stomach, still missing the daughter she never knew.

It was New Year's Day several years later, a happily married Diane was feeling kind of down about the weight she had put on over the years. The years of inattention to her body had pushed her up to nearly 200 pounds. She wanted to lose some weight but hadn't really considered how she would do it.

The answer was to come to her while talking with a bunch of her girlfriends. When the subject of weight

NEVER GIVE UP

came up, one of her friends told Diane she was on my program and that it was working great for her. "You really ought to check it out," she said. She explained to Diane how the program worked and the more she heard, the more sense it made.

Diane got a chance to hear more about my program when she caught one of my appearances on the QVC Shopping Channel. It was early January and I was talking about "new beginnings."

"I know, I know . . . the holidays just ended and you had more than your share of turkey and dressing, pecan pie and rum balls. But now is the perfect time to start! If you do start now, in January, why, you could lose forty or fifty pounds by summer."

Hmm, Diane thought. I suppose I could do that. And she listened on.

"But you've gotta start now! What are you waiting on? The ability to do it is inside you. Food has no power except for what you give it. Food will never solve any of your problems, past, present or future!"

Okay, that's it, Diane told herself. I'm going to do this and I'm going to do it for me!

Diane got my Deal-A-Meal program and took off at top speed toward her goal. She stopped dwelling on what she "couldn't do!" She found out she could do anything she wanted.

She dumped a lot of things including salt and sugar from her diet. She learned to really appreciate the taste of her food as she was cutting back. Diane began eating a lot more "fresh" vegetables and I mean "fresh." "No frozen or canned stuff for me," she said. She also exercised every day and watched with glee as her body size became slimmer.

Friends and co-workers were noticing her new look as well as her new attitude. . . .

"Diane, you're looking great, what's your secret?"

"Diane, are you really as happy as you look?" People seemed friendlier to her because *she was* friendlier! They treated her differently because *she* was different. I'd said, "If you start . . . in January . . . you can lose forty to fifty pounds by summer." Well, in five months, Diane had lost forty-eight pounds and she was moving ever closer to her goal.

Now that Diane had seen what she could do with her body, there was something else that had always remained heavy on her *mind*, the daughter she had given up twenty-six years ago. The weight loss had changed her so much that now she felt empowered with the courage needed to search for little Trisha who certainly was today a full grown woman. Diane had some *unfinished business*. She had actually placed her maiden name into Central Registry years earlier. The registry took personal information about the parent and matched it with information about the child who had been given up for adoption. The only thing was, if both parent and child didn't register their names, the match would never occur. Diane assumed that since she had heard nothing in all this time, the registry was not going to be the answer.

So she tried another way, enlisting the help of a "searcher." The searcher provided Diane with other ways of locating her child but that's all. Diane was told of the resources that would be helpful, but she would have to do the legwork herself.

She made phone calls, visited the courthouse to check adoption records and not only in her county but the county her baby was actually born in. She also tried to get records from the hospital where Trisha was born and came up with nothing on that

NEVER GIVE UP

end either. It was as if her child had never been born but Diane still wouldn't stop in her search.

Diane sat in the main branch of her local library going after another long shot. She had calculated from Trisha's date of birth to the year she would have graduated high school. The library had hundreds of copies of old area high school yearbooks and Diane painstakingly flipped through page after page in each one until she got to one picture, one picture that stood out from the rest.

It was a picture of a young girl, she must have been sixteen or seventeen but Diane was sure without a doubt in her mind that little black-and-white photo was of her daughter. She wanted to scream at the top of her lungs right there in the library, "This is my daughter!"

Diane knew she was close now. Starting with Trisha's last name, she made a series of phone calls to trace her family. She found out that Trisha's real name was now Cheryl and that she lived in northern Ohio. That's where Diane was able to finally send a message . . . a message to Cheryl, the daughter she'd lost so many years ago.

It was days before Diane heard anything, every phone call that came in could have been from Cheryl. I've gotten this close, she thought, God, please let her call me, she has just got to call me!

When the phone rang at 2:30 in the morning, it jolted an already jittery Diane out of bed! She wasted no time, though, picking it up. "Hello?" she answered, her voice still not quite awake.

"Diane . . . is this Diane?"

It was a voice Diane did not recognize, her voice perked up quickly. "Yes, it is . . . who is calling?"

"Diane . . . my name is Cheryl . . . I believe I am

your daughter." Twenty-six years of wondering, regret and emptiness came to an end in one instant. Before she could say anything else, she cried. She and Cheryl talked on the phone for the next three and a half hours. And they made plans to meet on that next Sunday afternoon at Cheryl's adopted parents' home.

Diane could not have been more excited as she neared the address Cheryl had given her. She had taken time that morning to pick out the perfect outfit to wear and felt confident about her appearance. She'd lost a total of fifty-six pounds, and hoped to make a good, very important first impression.

Diane slowed down on the pretty, tree-lined street that Cheryl's parents lived on, holding the address in her hand, one by one, she checked the numbers. When she spotted the correct address, there was a pretty young woman standing in the yard. She appeared to be waiting for someone.

"Oh, my God," Diane said out loud to herself as she stopped the car, she knew who it was! She got out of the car and walked toward the young lady.

"Cheryl? . . ." she asked.

"Yes, yes, Diane. My name is Cheryl, your daughter!"

The two of them hugged each other for what seemed like, well, twenty-six years.

"All this time I wondered what you would look like," Cheryl told her, "And you looked just the way I imagined, you're so beautiful."

"Well, thank you," Diane said, "I think I look just like you."

"Cheryl," she continued, "I have something for you. For all these years I wondered what I would say if I ever found you. Gosh, there were so many things." Diane reached into her purse and handed

RICHARD SIMMONS'

NEVER GIVE UP

Cheryl a beautifully wrapped envelope holding a single sheet of paper. "It's a poem," she said, "I'll just tell you I called it 'Sunday to Sunday.' You were born on a Sunday morning so long ago and I find you again today on another Sunday."

Cheryl took the envelope and thanked Diane. "Let's go inside and talk, okay?"

"Sure," Diane replied, "But can I ask you one question before we do?"

"Anything at all," she answered.

"I mean for your whole life you knew nothing about me . . . and well . . . my question is what do you want me to be in your life now?"

Cheryl smiled, took Diane's hand and said, "I just want you to be what you've always been . . . my mom!"

SUNDAY TO SUNDAY

Sunday to Sunday is only one week; seven short days.
But twenty-six years passed between our Sundays.
I saw your precious face but once, through the nursery
*   window.*
Today I held your face between my hands and kissed
*   your tears.*
Yes, you should have been with me, and if I had the
*   power I would change it back.*
But, for some reason, God had other things for you and
*   I to do, to become, to accomplish.*
Our reunion has allowed us to come together not only
*   as parent and child, but as friends.*
Today I have released my guilt as I embraced you in my
*   arms.*
We have found each other and, in doing so, have found
*   ourselves.*

Sunday, March 6, 1966   Sunday, June 14, 1992
Your Birthday   Our Reunion

RICHARD SIMMONS'

NEVER GIVE UP

I have **blamed** many people and many things for my fat, but I must admit I **am to blame.**
I hold the fork.

◆

I **forgive** those who have made fun of me, judged me or put me down because of my weight.

◆

I **forgive** myself and **forget** about all the times I tried before.

◆

THE CONTEST

Marie's Story

I always try and make each of my exercise videos a little more exciting than the last. If you've seen *Sweatin' To The Oldies III*, you know we built an amusement park set complete with a merry-go-round, a Ferris wheel and of course the tunnel of love.

Several people I've gotten to know through letters and phone calls were chosen to appear on the video. They were flown out to Los Angeles to be dancers in *Sweatin' III*. Now what could I do to make *Sweatin' IV* an even bigger blast? How about a national "Sweatin' Contest!"

I chose QVC, the nation's number one shopping channel, to launch my search because it goes into millions of homes. I actually remember the day I announced the contest because I was so excited about the video.

Everyone entering was instructed to choose a song from one of my earlier tapes, learn the movements, videotape their performance and send it off to me. I told them to be creative and have fun! Each entry would be viewed personally by me and I would announce the winner on QVC in four weeks.

Marie also remembers the day of the announcement. When she heard it, she already had a couple of the *Sweatin'* videos and had lost fifty pounds exercising with them. She considered the contest a personal challenge.

Immediately she sought her mother's advice. The contest required some work and she wanted to make sure she wasn't way off base in entering it. Without hesitation, Marie's mother counseled her to *go for it!* "You have always been a spunky kid," she remembers her mother saying, "I think you can do it. You've always liked to dance, too. You have as good a chance as anyone else, Marie."

That same afternoon Marie went to a birthday party at her aunt's house across the street. All she could talk about was the contest and kept asking each person she talked to, "What do you think? Should I enter or not?" The family was behind her 100 percent.

The next day, while shopping for her father's birthday gift at Radio Shack, the first thing Marie noticed when she walked into the store was a table piled high with blank videotapes, *and* they were on sale! It was like an omen . . . a good omen.

The next step was a phone call to her brother, Richard, at college. Richard could always be counted on for "way-out" ideas. Marie explained to him that she was entering a contest to appear in Richard Simmons' next workout video and that she had to do something really outrageous in order to get my attention. She was sure I would be flooded with entries (and she was right!).

Not only did Richard agree to help but the whole family got involved. They helped Marie shoot a very clever opening scene based on "Star Trek" her dad had helped her compose (this video was a real family affair!). After that, it was "chorus line" time and Marie was on her own. She had learned the routine for "Do You Wanna Dance." Nervous now, she had everyone leave the living room, there was to be no audience for her screen debut.

Having cleared the room, Marie stood there with the remote control in her hand. Taking a deep breath, she clicked the camera on. As the music started Marie began her performance. She danced and sang her heart out, putting her all into the number.

The song ended, she caught her breath, smiled into the camera and repeated the lines, "Hi Richard, I'm Marie. I may be your biggest fan now but I promise you, one day I'll be your littlest!"

Marie's video made its way to the pile of videos stacked all over my bedroom floor. Since I'd announced the contest, over 1,100 tapes had come in! So far that day I had already watched everything from a woman dressed as a bird dancing to "Rockin' Robin" to a husband-and-wife team dressed as dalmatians doing "Born to Be Wild!"

I got to Marie's package, opened it up and popped her tape in my VCR. I knew right away, this was the special person I was looking for. I had hundreds more videos to view over the next several days but Marie's entry, with the little starship *Enterprise*, kept popping back into my mind. I narrowed my choices down to

ten, then five and at last just one. Marie was my winner!

I called her up to give her the good news over the phone. "Marie, I'm so glad you're home, it's Richard Simmons. Guess what . . . you won my 'Sweatin' Contest!' "

Marie answered, "Yeah, right . . . this is Richard Simmons . . . who is this really?"

"No, it's not a joke, Marie, I'm serious, this *is* Richard . . . your tape was my favorite, you're the winner!"

"*Whoever* this is, stop joking . . . you are *not* Richard Simmons!"

"How can I convince you, Marie?"

"Well . . . tell me about my tape."

I spent the next fifteen minutes playing "Perry Mason" with Marie. I described her "Star Trek" takeoff at the opening, her outfit, the song she danced to and quoted word for word the ending her father had written.

Finally convinced, she screamed the good news to her family who had no trouble hearing her all over the house! She told me her total weight loss now was sixty-five pounds and she was still losing. My winner was a "loser." I liked that!

A month and a half later, Marie had lost another twenty-five pounds, *ninety* pounds gone now and she was ready for her trip to Los Angeles. All along Marie had great support from her family and it really mattered. Now, her brother, Richard, joined her for the flight out. Marie was ready to be the star of *Sweatin' To The Oldies IV!*

After spending just five minutes with her, I knew I had made the right choice. I don't think she had any idea how much work goes into making one of

NEVER GIVE UP

my videos. There were hours of rehearsal, of taping and of course, plenty of sweatin'!

During the final day of taping as the band played "Someday We'll Be Together," I glanced at Marie's face. She was holding back the tears as the camera zoomed in for one last close-up. The song finished, the cameras stopped rolling and she walked over to me.

"Richard," she said, "I can't tell you what an honor it was for me to be a part of all this with you."

I had to tell Marie not to talk to me about honor. I was the one honored to have met *her*. It took a lot of belief in herself to send that video in to me. When *Sweatin' IV* was all edited and finished, then it was *my* turn to send a video to Marie. I wanted her to see how good she looked and hoped she would take pride in the great job she had done.

Marie didn't stop reaching for her goal after she got back home, either. She's lost even more weight, now 148 pounds lost! And to think she was so worried about winning a contest . . . truth is, she was a winner all along!

CATTLE CALL

Ellen's Story

I was preparing to do a new commercial and wanted to try a different way of recruiting. I needed five overweight women ranging in weight from 180 to 400 pounds and for a change I decided to hold an open audition, rather than picking the people from my exercise classes or the mail I receive, which is what I ordinarily do. I didn't think I needed a professional actress. My thinking was an overweight woman is an overweight woman whether she's an actress, supermarket checker or bookkeeper.

Over 200 ladies showed up for the audition. Ellen was one of them, an actress from New York City trying to make it in Hollywood. Reading for "fat parts" was nothing new to Ellen, it was her career!

If the part called for a 240-pound cashier or

someone's overweight aunt, Ellen's agent sent her out just as he did for my open call.

She arrived at the studio and was handed a copy of the script so she could familiarize herself with the lines when her turn came to go in front of the camera. She started to read the phrases on the page and was taken aback. There weren't any one-liner fat jokes or food jokes like the hundreds of auditions she had been on in the past.

What she had to say this time were things she had told herself so many times before. Things like, "I admit I'm fat . . . I'm addicted to food . . . I am to blame because I hold the fork . . . I'm going to try again because I am worth it!"

The more she read the script, the more nervous she became. Was this an audition or a revelation? Was somebody up there trying to tell her something?

Ellen's thoughts were interrupted by a stage hand's voice shouting, "It's your turn, Miss, come with me, please."

She was escorted onto the stage. "Just look right here into the camera and read your lines please, thank you."

Ellen was a seasoned veteran at these open calls which is why it was so strange that she was nervous. She began to read the lines. "I . . . I . . . admit I'm fat . . . and I . . . I . . ." she could feel tears start to well up. It was time to regain her composure. Pull yourself together, she admonished herself. You're a professional.

Starting over, she struggled through the words until at last she finished the reading. Glad it was over with, she went directly to her car and had to wipe away tears all the way home.

Ellen received word in a couple of days from her

agent that she didn't get a part in the commercial. She felt rejected and relieved at the same time. But though the audition was over and the choices were made, those words from the script stayed in her head.

A year passed and Ellen kept going on those open calls while managing the apartment building she lived in to earn extra income and a place to live. One afternoon, on the way to another audition, she was waiting at a traffic light when she looked to the right and spotted me waiting alongside her.

That's Richard Simmons, she thought. She briefly considered greeting me and telling me she had auditioned for the commercial.

We made eye contact as the light turned green, smiled at each other and drove off.

Like synchronized swimmers, we glided to the next stoplight and I looked over and said, "Hello."

Ellen smiled back at me and said, "Hi Richard, can I just say what a nice man I think you are? You do such great work!"

I thanked her and asked if she exercised regularly and she replied, "A little." To me, "a little" was always just another way of saying "No!"

I pointed out that my exercise studio, Slimmons, was only a block away and I would like for her to please come in one day. I promised her a free class.

The light changed to green and we said good-bye. I made a left to get to the studio and Ellen went on to her next audition. She told me later, that night at home she thought about our encounter as she reached into the freezer for that carton of chocolate chip ice cream.

What should she do, she wondered between spoonfuls of ice cream. She mulled the question around in her head for over a week before finally

NEVER GIVE UP

deciding to just pick up the phone and call Slimmons.

Soon thereafter, I went to Slimmons to teach one of my usual evening classes and when I walked into the exercise room, there was my traffic light pal, Ellen! "You're the girl from the red light," I said to her in front of the whole class. I was happy and maybe a little surprised, that she had actually taken me up on my offer.

Ellen laughed and said, "Don't say 'red light' too loud, Richard, . . . people will get the wrong idea!"

I was so glad to see she had taken that first step to come in and sweat with us for an hour. But I didn't want to get my hopes up too high for her. So many people come in, take one class, never to be seen again. I honestly thought Ellen would end up being one of them.

Boy, did *she* prove me wrong! Ellen was there for class on Thursday, on Friday, Saturday . . . in fact, she never missed a day!

The words she'd had to say for that audition had stayed with her all those months because they were meant for her—they hit home. Her faithful hard work has paid off, Ellen today is seventy pounds thinner! She no longer has to go on those "fat cattle calls." There is a little bad news though. Ellen's agent ended his representation on her behalf. "You've gone and ruined the look," he told her.

Ellen said, "That's just too bad. I guess I'll be looking for a new agent! I may still be waiting for that 'big' part, but at least I know that when it does come, the role will be played by a smaller, smarter and healthier Ellen!"

MIND OVER MATTER

I know I am thinner, the scale doesn't lie
and I suppose I'll believe it one day by and by.
When I look in the mirror (you may think I'm
    strange)
but I honestly can't seem to notice a change.
I'll keep on my program and watch what I cook
but when will my brain let me know how I look?

My friends are all saying I'm doing so well
"what a great effort" and "isn't it swell?"
My clothes are much looser, that's hard to deny
but it's still kind of hard to detect with my eye.
There's no information, no pamphlet or book
to inform when my brain will reveal how I look.

The tape measure shows that my size has diminished
the scale has pronounced that my weight loss is
    finished.
The evidence shows I have reached my goal weight
and wouldn't you know by a strange quirk of fate.
If seeing's believing and I'm not "mistook"
my brain has revealed how fantastic I look.

FRIDAY NIGHT FEVER

Marci's Story

*T*here was only one thing Marci had never told her husband . . . and I mean, never. That was how much she weighed: Marci was too ashamed.

How do you keep your weight a secret from someone you've known all your life? Marci and Ken knew each other from childhood. Marci could see Ken's house from the back of hers. They were neighbors before either of them could walk or talk. There was never a time in her life that Marci didn't know Ken existed and vice versa.

They grew up laughing, fighting and sometimes even hitting, but from the first day of high school, things changed. From then on, it was Ken and Marci together . . . just like Ken and Barbie. Their favorite pastime was dancing. Every weekend they would drive to nearby cities, visiting clubs to hear the newest bands, and dance the nights away.

At nineteen, Marci danced up the altar and became Ken's wife. She moved from her parents' right into her own home. By age twenty-three, she'd had three children. She gained fifty pounds with her first baby and continued to gain weight when her other two children were born.

Marci's first daughter was born with brittle bone disease. She spent many days and nights at the hospital with her baby. Marci would stockpile food in the hospital room . . . candy bars, cookies and other junk foods. Late at night she would snack while her daughter slept.

Marci's other "comfort zone" was the hospital cafeteria. She could never understand why people always complained about how terrible hospital foods were. She looked forward to the fried fish, fried chicken, the mashed potatoes and gravy which she found delicious. And eating in the cafeteria kept her close to her daughter which was also a comfort.

Even after her daughter came home, Marci continued to eat and gain weight, which made her feel depressed. She needed something to do to keep busy. Even though Ken had a full-time job as a steelworker, he and Marci decided to open a restaurant, a Mom and Pop kind of place.

Now Marci was around food all day long. Her mornings started out with frying up the hash browns and bacon. By lunchtime she would be flipping hamburgers and making chili. Of course, when she fried the bacon, she had a piece. When she lifted the basket of golden french fries from the grease, she sampled a couple.

Eventually, Marci's weight began to really cause her problems. She just couldn't handle the stress of constantly being around so much food. After living the life of restaurateurs for a year, Ken and Marci sold the business and she decided to spend her days at home with the children.

The only time Marci would leave her house was to go dancing with Ken, but now even that stopped. Whenever Ken would suggest they go out, she would have an excuse for staying home. She always insisted that he just go ahead and have a good time without her.

Marci's biggest fear and main reason for staying home was she didn't want to run into anyone she knew. She didn't want to be seen because she had gained so much weight. She had reached her highest weight ever. This was the secret weight she kept even from her own husband.

Ken never said a word about how much she'd gained. He never stopped asking her to join him on the weekends. But Marci always said no. That is, until her sister came to visit for a couple of weeks. She wasn't taking no for an answer and insisted they all go out together for a night on the town.

From the moment Marci walked through the door of the club and heard the music, it was like a flashback to her old high school days. She couldn't resist the music. Soon, she was out on the dance floor and to her *own* surprise having the time of her life, when from a nearby table, Marci overheard someone say, "Boy, look at that big fat lady, she really can dance!"

It took a moment for the stranger's comment to register. For a moment she'd forgotten, but *she* was that "big fat lady!" It was as if the floor had dropped from beneath her. She asked Ken to walk her back to their table. Marci did not feel like dancing anymore that night.

Slowly and sadly, Marci began to alter her life because her weight had brought her to rock bottom. Her daily life consisted of eating and watching TV. One day, flipping through the channels, Marci stopped at a show where I was interviewing a woman who had lost a great deal of weight. She put down the remote control, took her hand from the bowl of chips and listened.

"Richard, I couldn't believe how many grams of fat I was eating, *sixty* grams of fat, every day! I've cut that down to just twenty grams of fat a day now and I feel like a different person. You know, eating fat *makes* people fat!"

Marci couldn't stop thinking about what that lady had said. She wondered how much fat *she* was eating a day. After reading a few food labels in her kitchen and calculating a typical day for herself, Marci was surprised to discover she was way *over* sixty grams of fat a day!

On the next trip to the supermarket she decided to make some changes. Gone from the shopping cart were those foods laden with fat. Marci really began to think about just what she was eating. And it wasn't long before she could feel the difference. As she lowered her fat intake, she began to lose weight.

The woman on my program opened Marci's eyes. She knew now that eating fat *does* make people fat. Marci was no longer eating like a fat person!

After taking off ninety pounds, Marci wrote me a letter thanking me for giving her the motivation to change her life. I noticed from her address that she lived near Cleveland, Ohio, where I was soon to be appearing on a local TV show. I phoned Marci and asked if she and Ken would drive up so she could tell her story on the air. Marci was thrilled, and when the show began there she was, Ken by her side, right in the front row!

I was so proud when she stood in front of the audience, looked me right in the eye and said, "Richard, I'm Marci, thank you for inspiring me. I have lost one hundred and twelve pounds and I could never have done it without you!"

I got to spend a little time with the two of them after the show. You could see Ken's pride in what Marci had accomplished. His wonderful wife had gone from watching someone else tell a great success story on TV to actually being a great success story herself!

We finally had to say our good-byes. I had a plane to catch but more importantly for Ken and Marci, it was Friday . . . date night . . . a night for dancing!

THE RESCUE DOWN UNDER

Charmi's Story

*A*s a fat kid growing up in New Orleans, my physical activity consisted mainly of walking from homeroom to the cafeteria. When Charmi was a fat kid growing up in Illinois, her days were filled with ice skating, school plays and dreams of someday being a world traveler. Her weight never got in the way of her experiencing everything life had to offer. Her parents were very active, took her everywhere and never let her feel excluded.

As a 200-pound teenager she went mountain climbing in the Swiss Alps, rode the gondolas of Venice, skied the mountain slopes of Wyoming and even went hot air ballooning in Nebraska. Each time she took on a new globe-trotting adventure, she carried a little "extra baggage" on *herself*.

In the summer of 1988 something happened to make her change. She traveled to Australia, the

Great Barrier Reef. The day she was to scuba dive for the first time she and her fellow divers arrived at the docks and met the boat's owner who explained what they'd all be doing that afternoon, how the equipment worked and so on. He also issued wet suits to each of them.

When it came Charmi's turn to be fitted for a suit, the captain gave her a rather long look up and down then handed her his largest suit. In front of everyone, she sat down and attempted to squeeze her 267 pounds into the rubber outfit. She took a deep breath, held in her stomach, yanked, tugged and pulled but it was no use, it wouldn't fit!

Charmi brushed her dilemma off with a nervous laugh trying her darn best to make light of the situation. "Oh, I don't really need it anyway," she said, "I can go into the water with just my swimsuit on." Charmi was too amazed by what she saw to be bothered by the cold. All the colors of nature swam before her eyes. The coral was dazzling, the array of sea life swimming all around her appeared in never ending variety. She felt like she was in another world. As Charmi explored the reef, she was able to forget all about the embarrassing episode back at the dock. That is, until it was time to return.

She could have remained underwater for hours but it was time to get back to the boat and head for home. Charmi surfaced near the boat and prepared to reboard. All her shipmates got back on deck with ease. But Charmi was having a difficult time lifting herself up out of the water! The owner, seeing her struggle came over to lend a hand.

Charmi couldn't believe this was happening. I wonder how far we are from the shore, she thought. I'd rather swim than have to get back on that boat!

The situation got worse, one of the other divers realized the captain couldn't pull Charmi up alone, so he joined the effort. The two of them pulling together were finally able to get a very mortified Charmi safely back on the boat.

Everyone made a big fuss as Charmi tried to assure them that she was okay. But she was NOT okay! It wasn't okay that she didn't fit into the wet suit, it wasn't okay that she couldn't lift herself out of the water, it was not okay anymore that Charmi was fat!

When she got back home to Illinois, Charmi was still stinging from her "disaster at sea." Her mind was made up to lose weight. She tried group nutritional meetings and searched the library for diet books and had limited success off and on. But she felt like she was moving in the right direction and was keeping a positive attitude about the job she knew had to be done.

That new attitude was threatened after Charmi got to work one morning. She'd come in at 7:30 A.M. just like always but by lunchtime, she was out of a job. The company she worked for had changed management and in the process her position had been eliminated. Great, she thought. Now I'm fat *and* fired!

Charmi was determined not to let the bad news stop her efforts to lose weight. She went home and right away grabbed the newspaper to begin the search for a new job. Thumbing through the paper, she noticed a few ads for weight loss programs, stopping to read a bit of each one.

Later, she would tell me how she finally got to us. "I saw an ad announcing an upcoming personal appearance Richard Simmons was making in the area. I decided it might be worth a look. Was he for real or just a TV guy?" (So, Charmi—am I real or what?!)

I remember the day Charmi and I first met. I was busy signing autographs and talking one-on-one with the people who had come out to see me. I noticed this one overweight young lady standing off to the side. It's not like she was waiting to see me as much as she was just watching, listening and observing.

I called her over and we talked. I gave Charmi as much encouragement as I could then signed a picture of me to put on her fridge. She laughed when I told her my photo would scare away the calories. I returned to Illinois every couple months. Each time, Charmi would come and pay me a visit. I noted that as she lost weight, she became more outgoing.

Six months later after I first met her, I was in Illinois again and thrilled to see that Charmi had lost twenty pounds by following my food program!

I had her join a group onstage with me so we could all work out to a great song together. Charmi caught on fast, it was like putting a quarter in a jukebox, this girl could move and I could tell she was hooked on sweatin'!

I was to find out later just how "hooked" she was. After losing seventy pounds, she made a trip out to Los Angeles to visit me at my studio. She told me there was a new goal in her life and that was to become an aerobics instructor.

Charmi was serious about her new goal, wasting no time in getting certification to teach. She got a new job teaching at the local YWCA and today even has her own business appropriately called No Limits! The girl who never let fat get in her way decided to just *get* the fat out of her way! I think this poem she

wrote after reaching her goal sums things up very nicely:

I am sitting here, eyes filled with tears,
Today I realized a dream I've held in my heart for
  years.
I've spent years in a body that really wasn't me.
Now I'm here for all to see.
While it took some time, it was worth the wait,
I feel so alive, so free, so great!
One hundred and twenty pounds have slipped away,
I now look forward to every day.

P.O. BOX 5403

Marilyn's Story

*L*etters, boy do I get letters! From all fifty states, Canada, even some countries I've never even heard of. Some of them come to me through QVC, some come directly to my home, some arrive from my health club in Los Angeles. And then there's P.O. Box 5403 in Beverly Hills. I've been receiving mail at that post office box ever since I made "diet" a *real* "four letter word." That was over ten years ago and since the very beginning, one lady has made sure that every single one of your letters (no matter which address you write me) has made it to my desk. Her name is Marilyn, she's worked with me longer than anyone else and I wanted to introduce you to the woman who makes sure that I stay connected with all of you.

By evolution, by chance, call it what you want, but almost always the people who work with me either have or have had a weight problem. (Same thing, right?) Marilyn is not an exception, when we met each other, she weighed over 280 pounds.

October 1, 1980, Marilyn canceled the usual Wednesday night out with one of her best friends. She felt tired that evening and wanted to stay home. She wasn't too tired to cook herself dinner, though . . . mmm, Marilyn sat down to enjoy a meal fit for a queen.

She flipped the TV on to see if there was anything interesting to watch. The set was on channel four and that's where she left it. Hey, who wanted to get up and look for the remote control, dinner was waiting.

Back in the early 80s, there was a TV show called "Real People," I'm sure most of you remember it. For those of you who don't, each week the show spotlighted people from around the country who had unusual talents, were hometown heroes or who did special things for others. It was a showcase for personalities.

The night Marilyn was watching and eating, "Real People" had me on as one of their guests. Those were my early years, before a lot of you knew who I was and Marilyn certainly hadn't heard of me either. ·

The show came to my studio in Los Angeles, it was so new then, you could almost still smell the paint. They videotaped footage of me and my class going through our workout and there were several ladies who weighed over 200 pounds. They weren't shy, though. The ladies were in their tights and leotards doing a fine job, thank you, of keeping up with thinner members in the class. Jeez, Marilyn thought, they got a lot of nerve going on TV dressed like that, and jumping around, too. She went back to the kitchen to grab another slice of rye bread.

As she sat down to finish her meal, the "Real People" hosts were interviewing me. It was one of my first opportunities to address a national audience about the importance of maintaining a healthy lifestyle. I wanted America to see and know then, as well as now, that you don't have to be ashamed of being overweight. My other point was that while you're losing weight, you can have fun doing it, as we had shown in our exercise class.

After my interview, we brought on a few of those ladies Marilyn thought "nervy." They lined up onstage and we went down the line asking how much weight each of them had lost, "Fifty pounds, sixty-five pounds, seventy-three pounds . . ." Marilyn wasn't making fun of them now!

She wiped a morsel of mashed potato from her mouth and gave the fork a rest for a minute. Marilyn thought about all the meetings, doctors and hypnotists she'd been to, trying to lose weight. And there was the time she ended up in the hospital from trying to get thin by using diet pills.

When she was a little girl, her daddy called her "Kitten." She was one of the most popular girls at Fairfax High. She and her girlfriends chased boys and because they lived in Los Angeles, every star in Hollywood from Elvis to Pat Boone (you should see her photo album!). Yep. Marilyn was popular, fun to be around . . . and thin.

After high school, she fell in love with a young, handsome serviceman who stole her heart. He'd promised that someday they'd be married but never kept that promise. When he left the city with another girl on his arm, Marilyn was deservedly crushed. That's when a new Marilyn began to emerge; one

NEVER GIVE UP

who cried over the boy that got away and allowed food to take his place.

What started out as consolation for a broken heart snowballed into an obsession. Food became the focal point of her life. She still remembers going to some of the bakeries at Farmer's Market and ordering a huge cake. She'd have the baker spell out a greeting with the icing. "Happy Birthday, uh . . . Linda . . . yeah, that's it . . . Happy Birthday, Linda! She's a friend of mine," she'd tell him. But, oh no, Marilyn's "friend" was inside the big pink box she carried out of the bakery. (Next week would be *Jan's* birthday.)

Another of her favorite diversions was appearing at fast-food drive-up windows. That way the person taking the order couldn't see how fat she was until she drove around to pay for her order.

"Yeah, let's see . . . two chiliburgers, one french fries, no . . . make that two fries, gosh . . . I wish the people back in my office would learn how to write!"

But there was no one waiting for lunch back at the office, both burgers and fries were for Marilyn to enjoy, half for the drive back to work, half for when she got there.

As the segment about me on "Real People" ended, Marilyn stared blankly at the Chevrolet commercial that followed, then looked at the plate she had just scraped clean. I guess I could call this guy's studio, she thought. It's only ten minutes away from my house. . . . Well, I'll think about it.

The next morning, Marilyn had breakfast with the friend she had canceled on the night before. As they were dining and having a grand old time, the waitress brought their check over. As she laid the bill on the table, she looked at Marilyn curiously and asked,

"I've been dying to ask you this . . . weren't you on 'Real People' last night exercising with a bunch of other ladies?"

Marilyn nearly choked on her cheese omelet. Do I really look like one of them, she thought. Have I gotten that fat?! She knew the answer to that question. Excusing herself from the table, she went directly to the restaurant pay phone, "Yes, operator, I need the number for Richard Simmons' health club . . . now!"

I had everybody kicking up their heels to the theme from *Chorus Line* when Marilyn made her first visit. She didn't take the class but watched as we all pushed, lifted and crunched our way through a fun but grueling workout. Afterward, she walked over to me and introduced herself, "Hi, my name is Marilyn, this is my first time here . . . HELP!"

I gave her a hug and a kiss and said, "We're family here. We all motivate each other and you're going to lose this weight. We'll help you. I know it can be done because I've done it myself. I have lots of faith in you but I want you to have faith in yourself."

Marilyn knew it was time and she was ready to give it her best try. She got on my food program. (We called it the Live-It plan in those days.) She took the sweets, fats, red meats and starches out of her life. She found great new ways to prepare old favorites like fish and chicken *and* she discovered a potato doesn't have to be drenched in cheddar cheese to taste good.

Starting out with light aerobics activity, she did a little more each day working up to a vigorous five-day-a-week exercise routine. In one year she took off eighty-nine pounds and found a girl she hadn't

63 RICHARD SIMMONS'

known since the time she was crashing parties at Troy Donahue's house.

Marilyn should have been enjoying better times all around but there was trouble brewing at work. Most of her co-workers were overweight and as long as she was fat, too, everyone had gotten along great. But as her new look began to emerge, tension developed between her and her fellow employees.

"Oh, you think you're so much better than us since you've lost a little weight," they would say.

"Marilyn, I don't like this new attitude of yours, you were a nicer person before you started your stupid diet!"

Instead of cheering her on, the other ladies at work tried to make her feel bad for her accomplishment. It got so she absolutely dreaded going into work after a while.

How unfair! Marilyn had worked so hard and now she couldn't enjoy her own success because the people she considered her friends were treating her like the enemy. Marilyn's feelings were hurt and it showed. She must have had a particularly bad day at work when I saw her at the studio one evening.

"Marilyn, what's wrong?" I asked her before we started class.

"I don't understand it! You do something to try and improve your life and what do you get? *Rejection*, that's what! I've had enough rejection in my life!"

After she explained the way she was being treated, I asked Marilyn what she did for a living.

"I'm a secretary at an advertising agency in Hollywood," she said.

"So you type, huh?"

"Are you kidding," she told me, "One hundred ten words a minute."

Hmm, I thought, I just may have the answer for this one. After my appearance on "Real People" as well as my ongoing appearances on "General Hospital," the amount of mail I was receiving was picking up fast. You can write just so many letters by hand before your fingers lock in the writing position. The cramps you get are awful. I needed someone with Marilyn's talents.

"Well, give that advertising agency two weeks notice, honey, because you're coming to work for me! I'll talk while you type."

I hired Marilyn as my personal secretary just in the nick of time. After I went on the air with "The Richard Simmons Show," the postal floodgates opened up and Marilyn was my lifesaver. She could actually type faster than I could talk . . . imagine that!

She continued eating right and taking class and I was very proud when she reached her goal, losing 154 pounds. She was healthy and happy and I was delighted to have her working for me. But that's not the end to Marilyn's story.

Over the years I never stopped marveling at her typing skills and speed. When I noticed her taking breaks more frequently and doing little hand exercises, I asked if I was going too fast and if she was okay. "Oh no, I'm fine. It's just my hands get a little numb sometimes, and I get this tingling. I'll be okay, just give me a couple of minutes."

The breaks became more frequent and I became more concerned. I suggested Marilyn see a doctor, thinking she might have a little arthritis in her hands.

After a few examinations, Marilyn's doctor came back with a shocker—she had developed multiple sclerosis. The news was so unbearable that Marilyn spent days in isolation and depression. She continued

NEVER GIVE UP

coming in for work but she was like a different person. Everyone on the staff of my show was concerned about her and we all did our best to cheer her up. We didn't have much success in trying but Marilyn had found a way to ease her gloom. She turned to food again.

The old Marilyn was back and she ate with the same intensity and thoughtlessness as she had before. No one said anything about her increasing weight. At least she seems happier now, they thought. Besides, it's tough to say to someone, "Hey, aren't you putting on weight?" (We all love that question, don't we?)

Like everyone else, I too tiptoed around the weight issue. I'd drop little hints now and then, being careful not to upset her. Her multiple sclerosis was a mild case and she still worked so hard on the mail with me, there was no way in the world I would hurt Marilyn.

In just a year's time Marilyn regained almost 100 pounds and losing weight seemed to be the farthest thing from her mind. She was rarely in class, she kept snacks in her desk all the time. Finally I couldn't stand by anymore, watching her erase all of her hard work. I realized that I was wrong to bite my tongue for so long. I had become a "silent partner" to her self-destruction.

When I walked into her office she made a helpless attempt to cover the unfinished burrito on her desk. "Never mind the burrito, Marilyn," I said, "we need to talk. Please tell me why you're doing this to yourself."

"Oh boy," she said, "I knew this was coming . . . I, uh . . . I don't have an answer, Richard. But I guess it started when I found out about the MS."

"Marilyn, I know it's scary for you but it doesn't have to be. I told you when we first met that you were part of a family and it's still true today. All of us are on your side. We're not going to let you face any problem alone. Letting yourself go like this . . . what's it going to do but make your health worse? After helping me all this time, I would think you'd know that better than anyone."

I could see that she was about to cry. I got up and put my arm around her, "I want you healthy again, Marilyn, you remember how you felt after losing that weight, don't you?"

"Boy, do I," she laughed and cried at the same time.

"Well, let's bring that Marilyn back," I said, "We all want you back, honey."

After I left her alone, Marilyn dumped the rest of her burrito into the garbage. The next day, she was back in class, grunting and puffing. I'd seen that undaunted effort before. She's going to make it, I thought. She knew the prescription for her cure and she used it daily. Within another year, she was almost back to 126 pounds, but not quite. She was too thin at that weight anyway. She bottomed out at 155 pounds and looked and felt better than ever.

It's been twelve years since "Real People" first aired and Marilyn is still banging those IBM keys for me. She's got one of those fancy electronic models now though, a lot easier on her hands. Her multiple sclerosis hasn't progressed much, she still zips out letters with lightning speed.

In the years that have passed since her diagnosis, her weight has been up and down the scale. Sometimes when she's not feeling well, she still indulges her appetite for a quick "pick me up." Today she still

RICHARD SIMMONS'

NEVER GIVE UP

weighs about 180 pounds. (She'll get me for telling you that!)

There are some who would say, "Well, isn't she a failure? There's no success in her story." Oh, but there is, Marilyn has *kept off* over 100 pounds all these years and there is plenty of success in that fact. I think she has plenty of reason to feel proud.

She still comes to class at Slimmons and even though her balance and coordination aren't what they once were, she is there giving her best effort. She may overeat now and then but never let it be said that she's not eating healthy. She only shops at health food stores where she purchases organically grown fruits and vegetables and if that label doesn't say NO PRESERVATIVES, it ain't going into *her* shopping cart.

Some days she'll come into the office carrying an armful of mail and proclaim, "I've lost eleven pounds!" And don't you dare doubt her because she keeps a scale underneath her desk to convince the unconvinced!

Sweet Marilyn, where would I be without her. My friendship with her is a constant reminder that we are all part of a family. There is a little bit of Marilyn in all of us, some days the scale loves us, some days it doesn't. But through it all, she refuses to say, "I quit!" She keeps right on trying.

She's the perfect lady for the job because she's right there with the rest of us. If you ever want to say hello, drop her a note at P.O. Box 5403.

SWEET VICTORIES

Have you just got a minute? I am dying to say
Something totally thrilling has happened today.
I went to a movie, which wasn't the best
But wait till you hear what I've got on my chest.
I'm bursting to tell, it's a big deal for me
And once I explain I am sure you will see.
I guess you could say I am now in my prime
'Cause my legs could be crossed for the very first time!
I'm always afflicted with feelings of gloom
When I sit in a space where there's not enough room.
So today is a victory, a freedom of sorts
With legs I can cross, I may just buy some shorts.

HIS AND HERS SCALES

Mark and Sheila's Story

*M*ark would never let his wife Sheila bring a scale into the house. In eleven years of marriage she got blenders, toasters, even a big screen TV, but never a scale. Mark didn't want to know his weight nor did he want to know Sheila's!

When they were married, the two of them weighed in at a twin 180 pounds plus. From day one it was an easy journey into the 200-pound range and beyond. But as far as Mark was concerned, neither he nor his wife were fat, it was the rest of the world that was too skinny!

And with that attitude Mark was certainly in the right line of work. He managed restaurants for a living. Needless to say, he and Sheila enjoyed plenty of low cost evenings dining out and gosh . . . it didn't cost them very much, except maybe their health.

Sheila may not have liked Mark's point of view but she certainly understood it, probably because she shared Mark's problem. He had always had a weight problem and for most of his life had been made fun of and treated badly because of the way he looked.

But Sheila had reached a point where she had to separate herself from her husband's problems. She had become extremely unhappy with her own appearance. From time to time when they were watching TV together and saw one of my commercials, Sheila would seize the opportunity to ask Mark again if she could bring a scale into the house and he'd always tell her the same thing, "No, we *don't* need a scale!" Respecting his wishes, Sheila would keep the peace and drop the subject for a while just like she always did.

On one occasion, Sheila had a chance to watch one of my commercials alone while Mark was away. She watched and listened carefully as one success story after another told of their new, more active life-styles as a result of losing weight. "That's it," Sheila decided. "I'm ordering a Deal-A Meal for myself!"

Sheila watched for the delivery truck every day until her package arrived. She was filled with excitement, eager to get started when it got there but realized a very important item was missing to chart her progress . . . a scale! She had to make her purchase in secret and felt bad about doing something behind Mark's back but losing the weight had become that important to her.

Armed with her new weapons for fat fighting, Sheila readied herself for the battle against the pounds! Each day she faithfully followed the food program and at night would weigh herself in secret then put the scale away where Mark would never find it. As her work started to pay off and she was losing weight, she was elated! Her only regret was not being able to tell Mark. Well, it turns out she didn't *have* to tell him . . . Mark began to notice the change in her appearance.

"Sheila," he asked, "is it my imagination or have you lost a little weight?"

Taken aback by his question yet flattered by it at the same time, she decided it was confession time. She told him, "Yes Mark, I have lost some weight, fourteen pounds as a matter of fact! Now wait here and I'll show you how I did it!"

After sharing my food program with him, Sheila brought out the really big secret—she showed him the scale! Placing it on the floor directly in front of Mark, she said as she got on, "I want you to see that you're not the only person in the world who's overweight!"

When Mark saw what his wife weighed, he just couldn't believe it . . . 333 pounds! Having blinded himself to their obesity for so many years, the truth was not so easy to accept.

Sheila stepped down, looked at Mark and said, "Your turn!"

Bracing himself, Mark stood on the scale and got the second shock of his evening, his own weight was 347 pounds! The two of them could not have planned it this way if they'd tried, identical weights on their wedding day and over a decade later, they'd gained an identical 150 pounds!

Mark and Sheila stayed up the rest of the night discussing what to do next. Bound and determined to reverse the damage of their undisciplined eating habits, it was as if another wedding had taken place. They vowed to lose weight and because they loved each other so much, they would do it together . . . one partner helping the other.

Mark woke up the next morning a changed man, telling Sheila, "We are going to do this!" He came home from work that night bearing gifts, not one new scale or even two but *three* of them! One for each of them and for each bathroom in the house!

No longer afraid, not only would Mark weigh himself on *his* scale but on Sheila's, too, for comparison's sake! The man threw himself into the task at hand. Of course, Sheila was delighted with her husband's new attitude. The original game plan was her idea but she had no problem with Mark taking over as "quarterback."

Weight was no longer the unspoken taboo word in this home, sticking to the food plan, comparing the numbers daily, they made a great team!

Mark reached his goal first, slimming down from 347 to 198 pounds in a year and a half. Sheila had lost 102 pounds and wrote me with rave reviews about the different husband Mark had become. "He looks great! He has so much more self-esteem now, he's like a whole new person!" Never thinking of herself, Sheila wanted me to call and congratulate Mark, which I was more than happy to do!

Mark shared a story with me. The two of them were at a carnival recently and while walking down the midway, Mark saw the Guess Your Weight attraction. He couldn't resist the temptation to have someone guess *his* weight . . . oh, he didn't care if the guy was right or wrong. He just wanted a chance to show off his new streamlined frame. My question was, "What ever happened to the guy who wouldn't let a scale into the house?"

Sheila still has some more weight to lose but she's

not giving up. How could she with an inspiration like Mark around the house? She's looking forward to losing those last pounds and until she reaches that goal promises . . . she will *never* "scale back" her efforts!

PRAY AND WEIGH

4:05 in the afternoon . . . Whoops! I'm late!"
I was selecting my music to play for the class I was
teaching that evening but I would have to finish
up later! I had a very important phone call to make
to my friends at the church.

Now, you're probably wondering, "What
church?" so I should explain. I had received a letter
from a terrific lady named Terry, she attends the
United Pentecostal Church in western New York.
Terry wrote me about herself and another group of
ladies at the church who formed their own support
group to motivate each other to lose weight. They
were all using my Deal-A-Meal program to get in
shape and Terry wanted to know if I could give
them a word of advice or more information to help
keep them going.

So you know me, I love making those phone

calls. Terry told me she had lost twenty-four and a half pounds so far. There were five other ladies in the group and they met once a week. Club dues were a dollar a week and the money was used to buy incentive gifts for every ten pounds one of the members lost. Every week one lady gets a chance to share ideas on helping the other members through exercise tips, testimonies of success, recipes, even Bible Scriptures. I thought they were all too cute so I asked Terry, "When's the next meeting, I'll call and we'll do a group meeting over the phone. This will be fun for all of us!"

Terry was thrilled, she said she'd even buy one of those speakerphone attachments so no one would miss a thing. "Only problem is," she said, "nobody will believe you're going to really call!"

"Well you tell them they *better* believe it," I said. Hey, I wasn't gonna miss this, not even for a one ton box of Godiva chocolates! The next meeting was Monday at 4:00 (my time) and like I told you . . . I was late! Did I tell you the name of their group? . . . It's called Pray and Weigh!

I dialed the number and heard Terry's cheery voice on the other end . . . "Hellooo!"

"Yes, is this Wong Fu's Chinese takeout . . . I'd like to place an order please!" I heard a roomful of ladies burst into laughter!

"Terry, is everybody there?" I asked.

"We're all here, Richard. We even added four new members so there's ten of us instead of just six now. But we got a little worried for a minute when you hadn't called at 4:00, we were just about to bring out the vanilla ice cream and chocolate syrup!"

"Oh please . . . don't do that," I said. "At least wait till I get there!" They laughed again, I could tell I had a fun but somewhat rowdy group on my hands but it was time to get a little serious.

I was holding Terry's letter in my hands when I called. Each of the ladies in the group had signed the letter with a little note to me. Virginia's name was first so I asked, "Where's Virginia, we're gonna start with you!" Everybody laughed at my calling her up first. "Why are you all picking on Virginia?" I asked.

Someone shouted, "Because she's the pastor's wife!"

"Ohhh, I see . . . Virginia are you there?"

"Yes, I'm here, Richard."

"Virginia, is it hard work being the pastor's wife?"

"No, I wouldn't say it's hard work. Actually, I really enjoy it," she said.

"And do you have weight to lose?"

"Oh yes."

"Okay, and how much?" I asked her. The room was suddenly quiet for a change. "Virginia, are you there?"

"Yeah, Richard, but are you going to ask everybody else that question?" There was laughter again.

"I sure am, now how much weight do you need to lose?"

"Well, I'd figure at least one hundred pounds."

I asked her, "What's the biggest obstacle in losing the weight?"

"Oh, I'd say the traveling I do with my husband. I can do pretty good up until about April but that's when his travel season starts and the next few months, it's really tough for me with such a crazy schedule."

"Trust me, I understand," I told Virginia, "I keep a nonstop schedule year-round but I always make time to watch what I eat *and* get in some exercise, too. That's what you're going to have to start doing. I'm a little worried about you carrying that much extra weight. As the pastor's wife, I know you probably spend a lot of time helping others. But now you've got to start taking time to help *Virginia*. What if something happened to you, we want to hold on to people like you in this world, we need more Virginias! I mean, you are almost like an extension of God here on earth. I want you to remember that as you lose this weight, okay?"

"You're absolutely right, Richard, about everything. And I've done real well losing this weight for a while but, like I said, it does get hard sometimes."

"Sure it does, but you know you can do it, so start proving it . . . please."

Diane was the next lady on the list so I called her name next! "Diane, how much weight do *you* have to lose?"

"One hundred twenty pounds Richard, but I've already lost thirty-seven and a half pounds!"

The whole room burst into applause and I joined them! Diane was forty-two-years-old and had suffered congestive heart failure. I asked if she was afraid of her condition.

"You know, I was frightened at first, but I've accepted it now. I'm not living in fear of it but I know I have to be extra careful."

"Do you think your heart problem is a result of you being overweight?" I asked.

"No," she replied, "my doctor said it was a hereditary condition."

"But don't you think you would feel better overall if you lost the extra weight?"

"Oh sure," Diane told me, "I already feel better

with the weight I have lost. I can't do your Sweatin' tape but I can do your walking cassette and I *do* take walks as often as I can!"

"That's great," I told her, "One more question . . . what'd you have for dinner last night?"

"I had broiled fish, a baked potato and fresh vegetables," she said. Diane was certainly on the high road so I checked for the next lady on my list. Now Vivian was the next name up but the first time I talked to Terry, she told me that Vivian had quit the group. I was surprised she was present so my first question was, "Why did you quit the group?"

Somebody said something in the background, I couldn't quite make out what it was but I did hear Vivian tell her, "Oh, I can't *wait* till he talks to you!"

"Vivian," I asked her again, "why'd you drop out of the group before, did you get a better job as a bingo caller?"

"Sorta like that," she said laughing. "Honestly, Richard, I just haven't been motivated . . . and I don't know why."

"How much do you have to lose?"

"Around sixty pounds," she said. "I lost twenty-five once, I felt a lot better then, too. I know I could do a lot better though."

"So, you're back in the group, that's good," I told her. "But don't get caught up in this lose-gain-lose-gain circle. You've got all these great friends around you, let them help motivate you, that's what your meetings are all about."

"I know, Richard," she said, "I know I need to lose, I'm really going to try and keep it off!"

"All right, where's Debbie?" I screamed!

"Wait, wait," someone shouted, "She's running the camcorder!"

NEVER GIVE UP

"Camcorder," I said, "This isn't 'America's Funniest Home Videos,' you know. Debbie get to this phone!"

"Hi, Richard, I'm here," Debbie said, "you'd be real proud of me, I've lost one hundred pounds!"

I was waiting for the customary applause but there was none!

"Gotcha, I'm just teasing ya," she said.

I suggested we all bow our heads in prayer, "Dear heavenly Father, forgive Debbie for . . ." I cut the prayer short to ask Debbie how much she really had to lose and "no more pranks!"

Debbie explained that she only had thirty pounds to take off and that before she'd gained the weight, she'd always been very thin.

"So, where'd the thirty pounds come from?" I asked. "Did you find it under a pew?"

"I got pregnant," she told me, "I'd always really wanted a baby and when I finally was expecting, well, because I was so thin, no one believed me, not my mother-in-law, not even my own mother. So I ate and ate and then finally they believed me after I got fat. But the bad news is once I started, I couldn't stop eating and here I am today thirty pounds overweight."

"And *today* is the day to start, too," I said. "So you have just the one child now."

"No," Debbie said, "I have three."

"Three kids, and you work every day?" I asked.

"Nope, I'm at home during the day."

I told Debbie to start right away working on that thirty pounds and to take time for herself from what I'm sure were busy days taking care of those three kids. "They're going to need and want a healthy mom as they grow older, and I know you want to be there for them. Now, who else is there?" I asked.

Like a choir of angels, they chimed in unison, "Joy!"

"Now, why is Joy so popular?" I wanted to know. It turns out Joy was Virginia's sister. "What'd you think about your sister marrying a pastor?" I asked her.

"Well, he wasn't always a pastor," Joy replied.

"What was he before becoming a pastor?" I asked.

"He was a plumber!"

We all laughed, from fixing pipes to mending souls, that was quite a leap!

"How much weight do you want to lose, Joy?"

"Fifty pounds," she said. "Well, I'd really like to lose eighty but the way I look at it is, once I lose the first fifty, then I can go on to that final goal of eighty pounds total."

"I like that idea," I told Joy. "And how are you doing now with your weight?"

"Well, I've been using my Deal-A-Meal every day and I've lost twenty and a half pounds."

Now we could applaud for *real* this time! Sounds like Joy is heading in the right direction and I had talked to my six original "Pray and Weigh" members.

"Now I understand we have some new sheep in the fold. What are their names?"

The "Angels" sang out the names, "Wendy . . . Sandy . . . Shelly . . . Anna."

I decided to start with Anna. "What'd you have for breakfast this morning?" I asked her.

"I never eat breakfast," she replied.

Before I could yell at her for skipping meals, someone shouted out, "She's Debbie's mom!"

NEVER GIVE UP

"Why, Anna," I said, "you could get on the program with your daughter, I get letters all the time from moms and daughters, even whole families losing weight together! What's your goal?"

"I need to lose fifty pounds," Anna said, "but I have a question to ask you."

"Go right ahead," I said.

"See, somebody told me that when you're losing weight, the third, seventh and eleventh weeks are 'danger' weeks. I can get past weeks three and seven, but I can't get past that eleventh week. Why?"

"Anna, I don't know who you're getting advice from but I sure hope you're not paying for it! When you're losing weight, your body doesn't know the difference between one week and the next. That's an idea you've planted in your brain. You're sabotaging yourself. That eleventh week idea is meaningless. We all go through rough spots, they're called plateaus. Think of yourself driving a car, there's a bump in the road so you purposely hit the brake to slow down. But losing weight, you're driving a different kind of car. Honey, when you see that bump . . . hit the gas and drive right on over it! Let's see here . . . where's Shelly?!"

"Right here, Richard!"

"So Shelly . . . tell me about Shelly!"

"Well, I gained sixty pounds with my first baby . . ."

"Yeah," I said, "And did you lose it?"

"No."

"What do you weigh today, Shelly?"

"A hundred and ninety-nine pounds . . . but I'm not ashamed," she answered.

Interesting response, I thought so I had to go for

the follow-up question. "You know a lot of people *would* be ashamed of that number, Shelly, so why aren't you?"

"Because I'm five months' pregnant!"

I told Shelly, "Just because you're pregnant . . . that's no reason to let your weight get out of hand. Are you eating healthy?"

"Kind of," she said.

"Kind of is not good enough, Shelly. Your new baby is depending on you *now*, *before* he or she is born. I want you to start concentrating on the way you eat. You've got a human life counting on you . . . you've got to be more responsible! Sandy . . . you're next, come to the phone, please, Sandy."

"Hi, Richard."

"How're you doing, Sandy?"

"I'm nervous."

"Well don't be nervous, honey, we're your friends. How much weight loss are you aiming for?" There was another one of those rare quiet moments at Pray and Weigh. "Sandy, do you have fifty pounds to lose?"

"More," she said.

"Sixty pounds?"

"More."

"Okay, one hundred pounds to lose?"

"More."

"Sandy, don't be embarrassed. We're here to help each other. How much weight do you want to lose?"

"At least a hundred and fifty pounds, Richard."

"As you look around the room, would you say you have the most weight to lose, Sandy?"

"Yeah, I'm sure I do."

NEVER GIVE UP

"Do you have children?"

"Yeah, six of them!"

"Gee, it sounds like 'The Brady Bunch' at your house!" I finally got her to laugh! "So, you're a very busy lady then, that's a lot of responsibility, but you've still got to make time for Sandy! God has blessed you with six kids and I want those legs to be able to help you keep up with them. And you won't be able to if you don't lose some of this weight."

"I do try," she said, "but having six kids makes it very hard. For one thing, they never like anything I cook!"

"What kinds of food do they like?" I asked.

"Junk," Sandy replied.

"Tell me some of the things you make for them."

"Well, let's see . . . chicken, they hate that . . . of course, they can't stand vegetables either but they do like fried fish sticks, pizza, stuff like that. And Richard, I can't eat what they eat and still lose weight!"

"You know, Sandy, actually you can . . . it's not what you eat so much as how *much* you eat. You and your kids can have the same things but you just have to control your *portion* sizes. Just remember to try and balance those meals so you get enough from all the food groups. Now what about exercise . . . are you exercising at all?"

"Not much, Richard. It would be a real strain," she said.

"Do you think you could walk for fifteen minutes a day, Sandy?"

"I really doubt it."

"How about ten minutes a day. Could you walk that much?"

"I don't know if I could or not," she replied.

"Sandy, I want you to try something . . . starting

tomorrow, say at noon . . . I want you to take a walk. I want you to set as your goal ten minutes. If you can't make that ten minutes, maybe you'll only make seven or eight but that's okay. But the *next* day, when noon rolls around, try it again. Maybe you'll make it to nine minutes, you know what I'm saying? Just keep building your endurance while you watch what you eat, you'll be amazed by the results.''

There was one more member to go so I called for Wendy to "Come on down!" Wendy said she was nervous, too. "And what are you nervous for?" I asked her. "Do *you* have six kids?" We laughed. Wendy said she only had two but they *equaled* six!

"How much weight would you like to lose?" I asked.

"Well, I started out needing to lose eighty-six but I've lost ten pounds so far." We gave her a round of applause!

"Do you work, Wendy?"

"Actually, I'm going to nursing school right now," she said. "I'm going to be an RN."

"What a great career," I told Wendy. "I have a lot of respect for people in the medical profession. When you finish school, you'll be going out in the world to help a lot of people. But I want you to keep losing that weight! You're gonna be helping others but I want you to remember something . . . God helps those . . ." (everybody said the last part together) . . . "WHO HELP THEMSELVES!"

"Now did we skip anybody at all?" I asked. "Is anyone else there?"

"Chad's here," someone said.

"Who's Chad?"

"That's Terry's son," I was told.

"Does Chad need to lose weight?"

NEVER GIVE UP

"Oh no . . . he's five feet ten inches and weighs a hundred and forty pounds!" someone shouted.

"Tell him to leave the room," I screamed back. The room was filled with laughter. As I knew they would be, these ladies were great fun . . . and we were getting ready to end our long-distance meeting.

I asked if everyone had a copy of my Project Me Passport—some did, some didn't. I told them I would send extra ones so everyone would have a copy. I'm sure they all knew the "Ten Commandments" and I told them the Passport is like my own personal "21 Commandments" to live by every day. They listened as I read all twenty-one of them out loud and they applauded after I'd finished.

"I don't know everything about your religion," I said, "but I was raised in Catholic school. One of the lessons I learned for life is that I have to be good to myself and good to others. I have to be fair to myself and fair to everyone else. Whatever our religious beliefs . . . I'm sure we can all agree that these are important rules we can all live by. Be good and fair to yourselves by taking care of these beautiful bodies God gave each of us. A lot of people use the word *miracle* very lightly but I can honestly say I see miracles almost every day. You can make your own miracle happen by not giving in to the 'temptation of the fork,' exercising every day and watching yourself become a healthier and happier person. Every one of you deserves that."

I asked Virginia to close our meeting with a little prayer but the ladies had a present for me first. They had taken one of their Sunday morning hymns and changed the words to represent their particular struggle. I can't tell you the words but the title of the song will say it all, "I'm Determined to Hold Out to the

End!" The nuns in *Sister Act* would have been jealous, they sang it beautifully!

The whole group joined in our closing prayer. They prayed that "with God's help we will all do better than we've done before . . . tomorrow we will wake up more determined than ever to be the very best that we can be!" AMEN!

RICHARD SIMMONS'

NEVER GIVE UP

APPLE FOR THE TEACHER

Anne's Story

*I*t was April Fool's Day but what happened to Anne was no joke. She had wanted all her life to be a school teacher and April first was the day of her preemployment physical for her new job as kindergarten teacher.

She watched as the examining nurse moved the scale's balance higher and higher, 150 . . . 200 . . . 250 pounds! Enough was enough! Anne knew it was time to stop being the fool and start being smart about her weight problem.

She went home and pulled out the largest trash bag she could find and emptied the cupboards of all those foods that had made her obese right down to the cookies and bags of chips. Anne's family had never seen her take such drastic measures before. Of course, they all wanted to see her lose weight, her father had promised to give her anything she wanted if she'd just get the weight off. She had toyed with one diet after another over the past fourteen years; starvation diets, restricted calorie diets, no eating after 9:00 P.M. but the best she could ever do was lose and regain the same ten pounds or so over and over again.

But there was a big difference for Anne on this trip down "diet lane." She had seen me on TV and got the idea to add exercise to the plan. That summer, she started swimming laps in the pool at her apartment complex. She had walked past that same pool many times before but never had the nerve to swim in front of the neighbors. But now at 6:00 each morning before anyone else was out, Ann made the sunrise swim a regular habit.

By summer's end, she had worked so hard that her swimsuit was too large for her to wear. Encouraged by her own success, Anne was bitten by the exercise bug. She bought a stationary bike and rode it faithfully every day after work and on the weekends. She went for a three-mile walk each day.

Within just eighteen months of her April Fools' physical, Anne had cut her weight in half going from 250 to 125 pounds! The whole family was elated with her accomplishment. Her brother, John, in particular was beaming with pride over his "new sister." Anne had used my program to help reach her goal but it was John who wrote me about her success.

He wrote, "I just wanted to let you know that with your help, my sister has lost a hundred and twenty-five pounds. She thinks the world of you but she's the shy type. So, I took it upon myself to tell you what a super job she has done. If you could please just drop her a note of congratulations, it would really make her day!"

I didn't feel a little letter from me was enough so I plotted one of my sneak surprise visits to see Anne. I called John and asked for his help. He was more than willing to be my accomplice. We put all our plans in place and chose Anne's classroom as the perfect place to pull off our mission.

With everything set, I hopped on the smallest airplane I'd ever been on in my life and headed for the small northern California town of Ceres.

I left the airport and drove directly to the school where Anne taught. Being very careful not to be spotted, I hid the car behind the First Baptist Church and began the short walk to the school.

My cover was nearly blown when someone recognized me and a small crowd began to gather. I explained to them why I was in town and said I needed their help to keep things a secret. By that time John had seen the little commotion brewing, came over and walked with me the rest of the way.

We reached the school with my cover intact, John and the principal led the way to room number 26. I peeked through the window before entering the class and there was Anne, sitting with her students gathered around in a circle. She was in the middle of reading to them, *Clifford, the Big Red Dog.*

I walked into the room while she was still reading. The kids saw me first and when Anne looked up from her book at me, I said, "Hi Anne, I've brought an apple for the teacher because I am so proud of you!"

Anne didn't say anything, I reached my hand to her and pulled her up from the chair. Still, not uttering a word, she put her arms around me and gave me one of the longest, tightest hugs I'd had in a long time!

I explained that her brother had written me all about her weight loss and I wanted to say congratula-

NEVER GIVE UP

tions in person. Now, I've surprised a lot of people over the years but I'm telling you, Anne was *really* surprised. She couldn't get past "thank-you's" at first and since she was so speechless I decided I would take over the class.

Taking the book from her hands, I sat in one of the tiny chairs and finished reading the adventures of Clifford to her kids. After that it was time for art class. Some of the children tried to make Play-Doh figures of my head but they were having trouble shaping my hair. They were saved by the bell for recess.

Again, taking Anne by the hand, we walked out-side to join our class on the playground. The kids looked as if they were having way too much fun so I had to join them. It was like catch-up time for me because I was always "odd kid out" during my own school days. I remember staying away from the play-ground so I wouldn't have to endure being teased and made fun of . . . but not today!

We played on the swings, the sliding board, spun the merry-go-round and played my personal favorite, tetherball! The second bell rang, ending recess all too soon for me, but we marched back to the classroom where Anne talked to the students about my visit.

"I never met this man in person before today," she told them, "but he's very special to me. He's helped me so much more than he will ever know. I'm very grateful to you, Richard!"

That afternoon had been so special for me, not to mention just plain fun! Anne and I managed a few private minutes together and I had my turn to say how special *she* was. She told me then a little more about herself. "I really can't believe you came all this way just to see me. I had two goals for myself before I was thirty. One was to own my own home and I'm

moving into it this week. And you've helped me with the other one, Richard—a new, healthy body to live in." After a teary hug and kiss good-bye, it was time for me to get back to Southern California.

I had been home only a few days when a very large envelope arrived in the mail from Anne's students. It contained pictures they had drawn of the day we spent together. There was also a stuffed toy animal from Anne, it was good old Clifford, the Big Red Dog!

Today, one year later, Anne is maintaining her success. Teaching was always her lifelong dream but she really began to enjoy life when she taught *herself* the most important lesson of all . . . to take good care of Anne!

NAME GAME

Fran's Story

*C*ome on, Fran, give this guy a chance, you'll like him. I know it. At least let me give him your phone number, talk to him . . . you'll never know if you don't!"

Fran reluctantly gave her best friend permission to have George call her. She had just ended a bad marriage and wasn't eager to start dating anyone at the time. But her friend was the world's greatest matchmaker and she gave in only because she knew her friend wouldn't take no for an answer.

Sure enough, George did call and they talked . . . about everything. "When's your birthday? What do you do for a living?"—the usual stuff and the conversation slowly eased its way toward food! Fran was surprised at how she opened up with this guy. She told him she'd just separated from a man who was not just her husband but her eating partner, too. "I'll be honest with you," she told George, "we didn't just love to eat, we were addicts!" She even told him, "I'm overweight but don't you dare ask me by how much."

"I don't care if you're overweight," George responded, "but I really would like to meet you!"

He's got to be kidding! Fran thought. How could she let him see her. She weighed over 300 pounds. "He'll see me that one time and I'll never see him again!"

But George was the persistent type. They had a couple more phone conversations and he kept insisting they get together in person. Fran thought she was being smart when she told him "Okay, if you really want to see me so bad, I'm going down to the 'Sally Jessy Raphael' show next Wednesday. I'll be in the audience, so you can look for me!"

"What are you going on the Sally show for?" George wanted to know.

"Richard Simmons is going to be on. I got tickets because they're throwing a big Sweatin' To The Oldies party on the show for him. I think it'll be fun. So look for me, okay?"

Fran knew the audience would probably be packed with hundreds of people and figured George would never be able to pick her out of the crowd!

Fran arrived to find the Sally studio filled with balloons and streamers. Many of the people in the audience were wearing T-shirts. Some of the shirts declared how many pounds the person wearing it had lost. And some of the T-shirts declared how many pounds that person *wanted* to lose. The studio was jumping with excitement as some of the oldies hits from my videos blared over the sound system.

Oh this *is* going to be fun! Fran thought. It was fun

for me, too. Sally's staff surprised me by flying in some of the people I'd worked with in losing weight. Some of them I'd met before but others I got to meet for the very first time!

I watched as one audience member after another stood up and told how much weight they'd lost, each time followed by cheers and applause. When they finished, we dealt with the other half of the audience, those who were ready to start losing weight. The celebration continued as we tried to motivate each and every person who was at square one, trying to take the first step.

Sally weaved her way through the audience, as only Sally can, and Fran found her standing just a few feet away. Having sat through half the show listening to all those success stories and to her fellow audience members speak about losing weight, Fran couldn't hold her silence any longer. She raised her hand. Sally noticed her and came over. "Hello, you want to stand up, dear, and tell us who you are?"

Fran was stunned. Now what? This was national TV. *What am I going to say?* She stood up and spoke into the microphone. "My name is food . . . and *Fran* is my problem!" And with that statement, Fran was in tears.

At first I thought she had simply misspoke, but no, she had said exactly what she meant to say. Food was not the problem, Fran was! I left the stage and went up into the audience to put my arms around her as she continued to cry. "Just let it out," I said. "Let it out, don't worry. You're with your friends here and we're all going to help you."

After the show, Fran was one of the first people I wanted to spend some time with. But I tell you, I had to wait my turn. She had half the audience around

99   RICHARD SIMMONS'

NEVER GIVE UP

her, offering encouragement, sharing their struggle. I was happy to wait until they were all done.

When we had our chance to talk Fran told me, "I've tried everything, Richard. I don't know what else I can do! I've had nothing but negative thoughts lately about life and living!"

I told her that it wasn't time to give up, it never is. "I want to get your address and phone number right now. I want to get in touch with you as soon as I get home." I found a pen but searched all over for something to write on. One of the staffers on the show tore a piece of paper from a script book and handed it to me. Fran gave me her address and I kissed her on the cheek. "I promise you I'll be in touch real soon, okay?"

I had a couple more cities to visit on my itinerary but I made sure I kept Fran's address in a safe place. For the next few days she remained on my mind.

Meanwhile, Fran's appearance on Sally's show had aired already and she came in from work to find a message on her answering machine. "Fran, this is George. I saw where Richard Simmons was going to be on 'Sally Jessy Raphael' . . . so I taped it. I watched the show, Fran . . . I still want to meet you!"

Fran couldn't believe it. He saw the show and he still wants to meet me . . . get out! With the ice broken for her, thanks to the miracle of television, Fran couldn't say no to George again. They met outside a restaurant in a local shopping mall where Fran discovered . . . George was overweight, too. They went inside, shared a bottle of wine and talked for hours.

Clear across the country, back in Los Angeles, I was frantically searching my suitcase, my wallet, my carry-on bag. . . . *Where is Fran's address? I know it's here someplace.* When I'm on the road, I often have people hand me their address on a sheet of paper or give me a business card. I pride myself on never having lost a single one and I couldn't break my perfect record—not now, not with Fran!

On the verge of giving up, I tried my address book for one more look, Maybe I put it in there, I thought. I flipped the pages. Nope, no stray piece of paper in there. There was a pack of sugarfree gum tucked inside one of the compartments of my address book. I pulled it out to have a piece while pondering where, oh where was sweet Fran. When I pulled the pack out, I also pulled out two pieces of paper . . . one of them was Fran's address. "Thank you, God!"

I called Fran up and we had a good, long talk. She told me of her history with food and her husband. "We're putting the past behind us, Fran," I told her. "Today we start your future." I sent her my food program, my videotapes and my belief in her that she was not going to let her appetite control her life any longer.

We talked once a week. Fran told me ever since that moment after the show when everyone put their arms around her in a show of support: "I felt a sense of self worth. It was a new feeling for me." Fran had a new gung ho spirit about her. And it turns out tackling her problem with food was not her only source of happiness. She told me about George.

Fran told me how they met, how he'd watched her appearance on TV, and about their first meeting. "He's a special man, Richard," she said, "I like him a lot."

I wished Fran the very best but I couldn't help thinking about the terrible marriage she'd just ended. Now with a boyfriend who also had somewhat of a

101   RICHARD SIMMONS'

NEVER GIVE UP

problem with food, well I had two simple words of advice for her. "Go Slow!" Fran assured me that she would be careful and after that conversation, it was a couple weeks before we spoke again.

The next time I called . . . a man answered! I thought I must have had the wrong number but asked anyway, "Yes, may I speak to Fran, please?"

"Sure," the voice answered. "Say, your voice sounds familiar, do I know you?"

"Well, my name is Richard," I told him, still a little surprised that he'd answered the phone.

"Richard Simmons, you're *that* Richard, aren't you, I thought I knew the voice. Hey, thanks for what you're doing with Fran. She's doing real good, she's lost fifteen pounds already. Wait, while I get her for you . . . Fran," I could hear him calling in the distance, "Fran, Richard Simmons is on the phone for you."

When she picked up, I said, "Honey, could you have moved a little slower? What, is he living with you? When's the wedding? I've got to rent a tux!"

Fran laughed and told me, yes, George had indeed moved in and they were getting along wonderfully. "I'm not getting married but I am happy, Richard. This feels right to me."

Well, who am I to argue with true love. I wished Fran and George the best of luck and congratulated her on losing that first fifteen pounds. We continued talking and writing to each other. Fran was losing weight, up to a thirty-pound loss so far and George had even lost a few pounds, too. Fran was like a bird that had learned to fly so I left her more or less on autopilot for a while as I moved on to help other people get to the point she had reached in her efforts.

My birthday came on a Sunday this year and I was in town so I did just like I always do on Sunday, made lots of phone calls. The party could wait until that evening. I hadn't talked to Fran in a while so I put her on my "will call" list.

When I phoned her house, I didn't think it was my imagination, but she was a little short with me and I wanted to know why.

"Fran, it's Richard. I was calling to see how you were doing."

"Why," she asked, "do you care?"

Had I called the right Fran? I couldn't understand why she was being so curt.

"Well, it's been so long since I heard anything. I figured you didn't care anymore!" she told me.

"Hold on a minute," I said, "this isn't a one-way street we're on here. Phone lines and the post office travel in two directions. What is this all about?"

It turns out Fran wasn't really mad at me. She'd had what seemed to her was a humiliating experience a couple weeks back. She and George had decided to take his parents down to the New Jersey shore for the weekend. Fran was nervous about meeting his parents but doubly so because she still weighed 300 pounds.

There they were, walking on the boardwalk as scantily clad ladies in bikinis walked and ran past them, one after another.

"I didn't need to be reminded by them, no matter how indirectly, that I'm still fat," she said.

Later, when they had dinner, Fran's aggravation with her size grew worse as she had to squeeze her body in and out of the booth at the restaurant. She could not have been more embarrassed in front of George's parents. "Whose idea was it to spend a day

NEVER GIVE UP

at the dumb old beach, anyway," she was thinking out loud as we talked.

Her depression grew steadily worse after they got home. She spent the next few days feeling just terrible. Standing in front of a mirror, she looked at her body and thought, why is this taking so long?! Why isn't this weight coming off faster? Why do I even bother? I'm tired of you, I am just tired of you! Fran screamed at herself.

"And what about today, Fran," I asked. "How are you today? Are you still on the program?"

"No, I'm not Richard. I'm not going to lie to you."

I asked Fran to think back to that weekend at the shore. "Did someone on the beach say anything to you about your weight?"

She answered, "No."

"Did George say anything that day?"

"No," again.

"Did his parents make a comment?"

"No, Richard. They never said a word."

"Then what was the problem?" I asked her.

"Oh, I don't know, Richard."

"All right Fran, I want you to think back even further then. Remember when you were on Sally's show with me?"

"Yes, of course I do," she said.

"When Sally put that microphone up to your mouth . . . I want you to tell me what you said."

I could hear Fran let out just barely a sigh, "I said . . . I said my name is food and Fran is my problem."

"So let me ask you again, when you went to the shore with George and his parents what was the problem?"

I heard another sigh, "Me . . . I . . . Fran was the problem, Richard."

"That's right, Fran, you *were* the problem but you're not going to be anymore! Stop letting what others only *may* be thinking about you *ever* stop you again. If you run into a problem, don't be afraid to let me know. I'm your friend, but you've got to make *Fran* your friend, get back on that program, get over this depression and let's make it work again, okay?!"

Fran agreed with me and we promised to stay in touch better than we had. It was still early afternoon so I kept on making my phone calls. About three hours later the doorbell rang. I wasn't expecting company so early so I wondered who it could be.

I answered the door to see a lady in a uniform holding an envelope in her hands. She was a little overweight and she rolled her eyes a little and said, "Oh no, I was hoping you wouldn't be *that* Richard Simmons! Western Union, Sir. I have a telegram for you."

I laughed and told her to come in. "Don't worry honey, we're all in the same boat." We talked about her weight for a few minutes and before she left, I gave her a Deal-A-Meal and one of my tapes. "Now if you really want to lose this weight, you can. Drop me a telegram and let me know how you do, okay?"

I walked back to the kitchen where I'd left the envelope. I was actually kind of excited. It's not often that I receive telegrams from anyone. The note was brief, but sweet:

ROSES ARE RED, VIOLETS ARE BLUE,
PHONE CALLS ARE SPECIAL WHEN
   COMING FROM YOU.
P.S. HAPPY BIRTHDAY,   LOVE FRAN

105   RICHARD SIMMONS'

NEVER GIVE UP

It became one of my favorite presents! I called Fran a couple weeks later and she wasn't depressed anymore. She'd started the program the day after my birthday but she hadn't gotten on the scale yet. She did say, "I'm really feeling great and I've started to exercise again. And George is doing good, too, he's lost forty pounds!"

I felt a whole lot better about my good friend, "Her name is Fran and food . . . no problem!"

Today I will make time for myself. I will eat healthy and I will exercise.

♦

I will not **ignore, hide from** or **avoid** food. I will **face** food and not lean on it.

♦

I realize food has **no power** and will never solve any of my problems—past, present or future.

♦

DELIVERANCE!

JoAnn's Story

*M*arlene . . . Marlene . . ." JoAnn called to her six-year-old daughter. "See if you can get someone to come over and help me. I feel really sick!"

She had been lying on the sofa and when she tried, she couldn't move. Every attempt she made was useless. It was as if a heavy weight were holding her down and at the same time she felt very dizzy and lightheaded.

Six-year-old Marlene returned as fast as she could with a neighbor who lived in their apartment building. She sat with JoAnn until whatever had immobilized her eventually passed. The incident came and went so quickly, JoAnn thanked the neighbor for coming over and dismissed the attack as a fluke, she felt fine once it was over.

She continued her daily routine around the

house until she had the same experience again . . . and again! The attacks would usually happen when she was all alone and though they frightened her, she didn't tell anyone about them. Each episode appeared and disappeared as mysteriously as they came on. But since she always felt like herself once they ended, she felt no need to alarm the rest of the family. Marlene also kept "their secret."

As the attacks became more frequent, JoAnn's secret became harder to hide. The continued trauma was causing changes in her behavior and personality, a fact that didn't go unnoticed by her husband, Larry. He discussed the changes he'd noticed and JoAnn knew it was time to tell him exactly what had been occurring. Larry told his wife that she shouldn't ignore something like this and insisted she see the doctor.

JoAnn had a very difficult time describing to her doctor exactly how she felt when the "phantom illness" struck. "It's very hard to breathe," she told him, "I feel totally helpless, it's like I'm completely paralyzed . . . I become crippled, I can't move!"

After many tests were performed, the doctor diagnosed JoAnn's condition as "chronic nerves" and put her on medication. He prescribed Valium. She was not at all satisfied with her doctor's evaluation.

Chronic nerves, what in the world does chronic nerves mean? she thought. And what is Valium going to do for what's wrong with me?

She longed for a more rational answer, JoAnn wanted to hear that whatever was bothering her could be cured. She didn't like the idea of being put on some pill only to camouflage what might be an even larger problem.

She and Larry went to see several other doctors

including some specialists but they all reached basically the same conclusion, JoAnn had some type of nerve problem and was going to have to learn to live with it for the rest of her life!

She refused to take the Valium and with time her condition got steadily worse. She developed an intense fear of leaving home for any reason. Any effort on her part to combat the fear failed. The fear and depression at times were overwhelming. The panic attacks, for that's what they were, had reduced JoAnn to a hostage in her own home.

The simplest of chores became impossible, Larry had to take over doing the grocery shopping or any other activity that required JoAnn to leave the house. All her clothing was purchased from mail-order catalogues, there was no way she was going into a department store!

Her world had shrunk to the size of the house they lived in and sometimes even the very house became an object of fear! That's when the urge to move would overcome her. It would not be uncommon for Larry to come home and have JoAnn announce, "We're moving . . . I've called a moving company, everything's packed . . . we have to leave!"

In a ten-year period the family moved over a dozen times. Larry gave up job after job in city after city always hoping that the next move might help bring back the woman he loved and missed so much.

Even when Larry became gravely ill himself, and JoAnn was told by the doctor that her husband might not pull through, JoAnn could muster the courage to visit him only twice at his bedside, though he spent weeks in the hospital.

The trips to the hospital, the constant moving, yes, JoAnn would venture outside the imagined security of home every now and then. But driving from place to place, there were strict rules that had to be followed on the road.

Once they were all in the car, no one could get out until they reached the final destination. When it was time to fill up, JoAnn made sure Larry stopped at a full-service station so the attendant could pump the gas. Bathroom stops were permitted only in the most extreme emergencies. The car became an extension of home, it was her protective bubble with the family members serving as security.

As her fears worsened, one spot in the house became most important, her special place on the living room sofa. There she would sit most of the day, constantly stuffing herself with anything and everything she could eat, even foods she had never liked before! JoAnn's weight increased consistently and she gained eighty pounds. Sure, she could see the weight gain, but it really didn't matter. With all her other problems she knew any attempt to lose weight would fail.

On what would be her final move, JoAnn sat in her new home and considered her predicament. Here she was in a new setting, on a new street where she didn't know anyone, with nothing to do but watch time and her life slip away!

She kept up with the happenings in the outside world by reading the daily newspaper and that's where she found a most interesting article. It chronicled the lives of two women who suffered from panic attack syndrome. That's me they're describing, she thought as she read on. At the end of the article was a number to call for more information. She wasted no time in calling, hoping, "These people could bring me out of this nightmare!"

JoAnn was given a time and place for the next

meeting. For the first time in years, she was *eager* to go somewhere! That meeting turned out to be a true revelation for her, at long last she had a name for what had been tearing her life apart: *agoraphobia.*

The symptoms of agoraphobia sounded like a chapter from her life: fear of leaving the familiar setting of home, fear of public places such as shopping malls or grocery stores, fear of open spaces. JoAnn had found the enemy!

She listened closely as one person after another stood to share their personal struggles with the disorder. It appeared that the common link between those who had beat it was that they'd taken things slowly, step by step: set one goal at a time, accomplish it, then set another goal and move on. The strength of others helped jump start JoAnn to fight, but she knew it would take her *own* inner strength to pull her through.

She started out by tackling the basics, moving around more inside the house. Walking to the kitchen, seeing the dishes undone, she didn't go back to the couch and wait for Larry or the kids to do it, *she* washed the dishes! From there she'd take on another job like vacuuming the house or washing the windows, "graduating" from one job to the next. She made those daily chores confidence builders edging her way back to reality.

Part of that reality was the undeniable fact that over the years of mental entrapment, her weight had leaped from 155 to 245 pounds! Losing weight was to be her final chore.

Flying high with her newly discovered will to win, JoAnn tackled her weight head-on. Using my food program, she learned to stop eating out of despair and started eating for health. She cut calories, elimi-

NEVER GIVE UP

nating her overindulgence of fats and sweets and she started a regular exercise program. She lost 115 pounds, settling at a comfortable weight of 130 pounds, actually 25 pounds less than the time of her first panic attack!

I read JoAnn's story with amazement and joy. If you could only talk with her on the phone as I have, you would know the excitement in her voice, the way she laughs, her overall *very* positive attitude betray the ten years of psychological torture she had endured.

It would be nice enough to end this story with JoAnn doing her own shopping again, leaving the house whenever she likes and sure, she's doing all that but that's not all! Here is a woman who was a virtual prisoner of her own mind who is now secretary/treasurer of her local chapter of Meals-On-Wheels!

Instead of being trapped at home afraid of the outside world, she delivers meals to strangers who are unable to leave home for any number of reasons. Now you may not be agoraphobic and trapped in your home but we trap ourselves in lots of other ways, *fat* being one of the most common prisons we create. JoAnn unlocked her jail cell by being brave and refusing to give up, two keys to winning that can be found in all of us!

SHE'S NOT HER
Lou Ann's Story

T'm proud when I hear about all of you losing weight, I'm also, of course, happy when you take off the extra pounds. But I never thought I would feel *guilty* that someone had lost weight on my program. Lou Ann got into a little trouble on a recent shopping trip as a result of losing her seventy pounds and I'll admit, I felt like it was all my fault!

Lou Ann did a lot of shopping at the Sam's Club Warehouse near her home in Houston. Sam's is one of those membership stores where you have a photo ID made when you join up. You have to present your membership card to the cashier before the sale can be made.

Lou Ann had loaded up the kids in the family car and headed down to do her weekly shopping. Those Sam's Club stores are like massive warehouses of groceries and other household goods.

Lou Ann fought the crowds with her three children tagging along and was glad when she finally made it to the checkout with a cart loaded to capacity with merchandise.

"How're you doing, ma'am," the cashier said, "May I see your ID card, please?"

Lou Ann pulled her ID out from her wallet and handed it to the cashier. The cashier looked at the photo, then looked up at Lou Ann and back at the photo again.

"Ma'am . . . is this you?" he asked.

Lou Ann was a little surprised. "Well, of course it is," she told him.

The cashier looked over the ID again, shaking his head as he looked back at Lou Ann. "I'm sorry, this can't be you, it doesn't look anything like you!"

Now Lou Ann had lost seventy pounds, like I said, but she didn't think her looks had changed *that* dramatically. But she had to admit, it was kind of flattering that her cashier was so confused.

"Sir, I promise you that the woman on that photograph is me! But I've lost seventy pounds and that's the reason I look so different!"

"Uh-huh," the cashier said. "Well, I hope you understand but I can't take your word on this. Hold on just a minute, please." The cashier picked up the telephone next to his register. "We need a manager at checkout number twelve please, manager at number twelve." His voice blared across the store's PA system.

"This is amazing," Lou Ann told the cashier. "I'm telling you that's me. I just lost weight, that's all!"

"I'm sorry, ma'am," he said, "but I'm only doing my job."

Two minutes later, the store manager walked over,

smiled at Lou Ann and asked the cashier, "Yeah Alan, what's cooking over here?"

"Well, this lady wants to make a purchase but I don't believe this is her picture on the ID card."

"Let's have a look," he said taking Lou Ann's ID from Alan. "I'm sorry for the inconvenience, Miss," he told her, "but you know we have customers who lose their cards all the time, this is for your own protection."

Some protection, Lou Ann thought, they've got me feeling like a criminal! The store manager repeated the double take his cashier had done and wound up every bit as unconvinced. "Ma'am, I'm sorry but I can see why Alan called me over here . . . do you have another picture ID?"

Lou Ann's nerves were beginning to get a little frayed, she had a grocery cart full of meats, frozen foods and dairy products along with everything else she wanted to purchase. And there was an ever growing line of impatient shoppers accumulating behind her waiting to be checked out as well.

Reaching into her wallet again, she pulled out her Texas state driver's license and handed it over to the store manager. But the manager *still* wasn't convinced! Lou Ann had just recently gotten her new license and, of course, the photo was of her new thinner self.

"Well, this is your driver's license, all right, but I still don't know about this Sam's ID." The manager even got a *third* opinion from another salesperson— "well, her hair is shorter here, I mean it *could* be her but I'm not sure."

"Look," Lou Ann said, "I told you I've lost seventy pounds! You ever heard of Richard Simmons?"

"Yeah," the manager answered. "He's that curly-headed exercise guy from TV right?"

"Right. I lost weight on his program and that's why the ID doesn't look like me! The driver's license is new . . . that's why it looks like me."

"So this Simmons guy's program—you're saying it really works, huh?" the manager asked.

"Do you think I'd be standing here having this problem if it didn't? What do you want me to do . . . go over to the pastry department, gobble a few dozen cinnamon rolls and come back? Then would you believe me?" Lou Ann could have been very angry but this was getting to be just too much fun now!

Her fellow customers were slowly trickling away from her line looking for a faster checkout but, hey, it wasn't all Lou Ann's fault! She had been using the same ID at Sam's for three years and *now* they decide she is actually not her!

The store manager finally gave in and okayed Lou Ann's purchase but told her, "When you come back, please do us all a big favor, ma'am, and take a new photo. It'll speed things up for everybody!"

"Thank you, thank you, thank you," Lou Ann said. "Now let me get out of here before my low-fat milk turns to sour cream!"

Poor Lou Ann, I thought when I finished reading her letter. I've got to call and say I'm sorry.

Her husband, Greg, answered the phone, "Oh hi, Richard, how're you doing?" Greg was all excited, he had actually gotten on the program with Lou Ann and had lost forty-three pounds himself!

"Well, congratulations to you, too, Greg!" I said. We talked for a few minutes and I asked if Lou Ann was home.

"Oh yeah, she's here but she had a little accident this afternoon."

Accident! Oh no, I thought, was this going to be my fault, too? Turns out it wasn't. Lou Ann had been out working in her yard when she accidentally disturbed a bees' nest. The bees were not happy and they had let Lou Ann know just that.

"Lou Ann, are you all right?" I asked.

"Oh, I'm okay, Richard, I'm still stinging in a few places but I've applied a few compresses and it's getting better."

"Good," I told her. "I was calling about your other mishap at Sam's a couple weeks ago. Who ever thought losing weight could get you into so much trouble, huh?"

"Please," she said, "*That* kind of trouble I don't mind at all, I had a good time!"

"And you're maintaining your weight real good?"

"You better believe it. I tell you, life is wonderful when you feel as good as I do lately. There's so much more to look forward to. I'm pushing forty years old now and sometimes I feel like I'm getting so old but then other times I feel so young. So most of the time I just don't think about age at all!"

"I feel the same way," I told her. "And what about shopping at Sam's these days, is everything okay now . . . did you get your new ID yet?"

"Yeah . . . but there's still a little problem."

"Oh no," I said, "I'm afraid to ask what it is!"

"Well, when the lady took my new photo . . . I blinked! So now when I go in . . . I hand them my new ID and I have to close my eyes. But at least now they know that it's really me!"

DIET PRO

Theresa's Story

Dear Richard,

I am sitting here and I can't believe that I am actually writing to you. I have never done anything like this before.

I was flipping through the TV channels tonight and I saw about fifteen or twenty minutes of your show on QVC.

I don't even know where to begin or what I want to say. I just had this incredible urge to write you. I guess I am just hoping that if I write you, I can once again get the motivation I need to begin losing weight again. I say again because I have done this so many times before. I just want to take it off and keep it off, which is where I always seem to fail.

I guess I can start by telling you a little about myself. I am thirty-four-years-old and have been married sixteen years. I have four children, two daughters and two sons. I also have a full-time job outside the home. My husband's job keeps him away from home the whole week. We only see him on the weekends. I also have in excess of 100 pounds that I need to take off.

I was *reasonably* thin when I got married, if I were ever *really* thin, it's been so long ago I can barely remember. I started having babies right away and never seemed to be able to take the weight off after each pregnancy. I have never really blamed the pregnancies for my weight gain though. I know I had then, as I do now, very low self-esteem.

After my third child was born, I struggled back and forth to take off the weight. Finally when that child was around three-years-old, my husband had an affair . . . supposedly because I was so fat that he couldn't bear to be around me. I was so hurt. It woke me up, though. My husband walked out on me. I took a long, hard look at myself and hated what I had become. I was in my late twenties and couldn't remember what it was like to look in the mirror and actually like what I saw. I couldn't really afford it at the time, but I decided to join a supervised diet program here in my hometown.

It was very hard but I was determined to take the weight off. My husband came back to me after a month or so. We decided to try and make our marriage work. Little did

I know at the time, but his affair continued throughout most of my weight loss. And the girlfriend was not even superthin, like you think she might have been!

Within six months I had lost ninety pounds. It was coming off pretty quickly even though I didn't feel like it was quick enough at the time. The next two months proved to be harder but I lost more weight, a total of 104 pounds and I had only five more pounds to reach my goal.

This may sound more like a soap opera story line but this really is my life. I worked very hard for the next three weeks to lose that last five pounds but I just couldn't seem to take it off. And I wasn't feeling well either. The reason I wasn't feeling well . . . I was pregnant!

I was totally surprised. We had been practicing birth control and thought that three children was plenty, especially these days! It's not that I didn't really want another baby, it was just the timing! I had lost so much weight and just in time to gain it back during the pregnancy. My priorities shifted from weight loss to baby planning.

I really did try to eat low-fat foods but the weight came back really fast and I was so depressed. My husband wasn't too thrilled with me, either.

In case you were wondering, my husband's affair finally did end, about the time he found out I was going to have this baby.

So here I was again, four kids, moody husband and most of the weight I'd lost,

NEVER GIVE UP

back on! The thought of going through all those months of dieting all over again made me more depressed. But again, I tried more diets only to fail, fail again and again! I just didn't feel like I could afford to rejoin the program I was on the first time around. How could I spend that money on me when I had four little ones to look after?

Right before the new baby's second birthday, I lost my job of ten years. I was unemployed for almost a year. I got to the point that I didn't care if I even left the house. I avoided my family and friends because I was so ashamed of myself. Then out of the blue, a job offer came my way. I told my husband that if I got the job, I was determined to rejoin my diet support group. Well, I did get the job and I did rejoin but again, it was so expensive. I stopped going and dieted on my own.

I did really well, I think . . . losing around eighty-five pounds in about eight months. Then I hit a nasty plateau that kept me lingering at the same weight for over a month. I even joined *another* support group but quit after becoming discouraged with them. Most of the group were older ladies who only went to the meeting for the social aspect of it all. They couldn't keep me motivated! Very quickly the weight came back on, pound after pound. I'm sure you've heard it all before.

Now if all that weren't bad enough, the worst was yet to come! Last Christmas was certainly not my happiest. By the time the holidays came around, I had gained all eighty-five pounds back and my husband and I were fighting constantly about my weight. The funny part is, even when I lost the weight, he always complained that I was not losing enough or I was drinking too many diet sodas or doing something else wrong!

I know that I have to lose the weight for me. But when all you hear all day long is what you have done wrong, it just gets harder and harder to focus on the right thing to do *and* who you are doing it for.

Anyway, getting to the point, my husband bought me clothes for Christmas. Of course every single item he got me was too small; he felt bad and I felt worse! We had a big argument on Christmas day about all the weight I had gained back and what a failure I am!

A few days later, we went to exchange the clothes for larger sizes. What a day of utter humiliation! My husband informed me that he had never been more ashamed of me than when he had to walk through that mall with me. I have never been more hurt in my entire life. I feel like my husband should love me for who I am inside—not just how much I weigh. No matter what kind of disagreement we have, it always turns around and becomes my fault because I am fat!

After the Christmas fiasco, my mom and I were talking on the phone. She was telling me all about watching you on a television

125   RICHARD SIMMONS'

NEVER GIVE UP

show she'd seen. She told me that she would buy me your Deal-A-Meal and video library if I would promise to start the program. I promised I would and she sent me the set.

The problem is, I can't seem to get the motivation to get started! I have listened to a couple of the cassette tapes but I just can't seem to get going. I think the reason might be I've lost major amounts of weight . . . *twice* now, not counting the twenty-pound losses here and there. I know how much time will be involved in losing the weight—not counting the "keeping it off" part. I know I will never again eat like I do now and I feel like I will never ever be able to live a normal life for the rest of my life. Does this make any sense to you?

I find myself doing the same thing as before, though. I am avoiding my family and friends. If I spot a friend on the street, I will go out of my way to avoid them so they won't see that I have failed again!

Am I hopeless? What will it take to make me see that I *have* to do this for myself, as well as for my family?

Thank you for reading my letter, especially considering the way I have rambled on and on. Again, thanks for listening!

Sincerely,
Theresa

Well, after "listening" to Theresa's letter, I wanted to call her up and have her listen to me. I tracked her down at work in her office.

"Hello?!"

"Hi, Theresa, it's Richard Simmons. I got your letter today and I wanted to call to see how things are going for you!"

"Get out of town!" Theresa replied. "When the guy at the front desk said it was you, well, I thought he must've just heard a name wrong or something!"

I laughed and said, "Theresa, let's get right down to business! From your letter I can see you've been through a lot of diet programs, some good ones, too! But my question is, with all this knowledge you have about eating right, why *can't* you keep yourself motivated?"

"Oh Richard, you're so right, I know how I'm supposed to eat if I want to lose this weight but it's almost like I have to be told exactly what to eat. I feel like I have to be watched."

"You don't have to be watched, Theresa, but if you need to have a food plan laid out for you, I really think you should take a closer look at my program. Where's your Deal-A-Meal wallet?"

"Actually, it's in my desk drawer here at the office," she said. I told her to take it out and let's set her cards up for a typical day. We went through each of the six basic food groups from dairy to meats. At the beginning everyone should be on the 1,000 calorie a day plan.

"Now because you've been on so many food programs," I said, "I don't have to tell you that 1,000 calories doesn't mean you have to feel like you're starving. The secret is to plan yourself three good, well-balanced meals, and a few low-cal treats

NEVER GIVE UP

throughout your day. Let's do a for instance. What did you have for breakfast today?"

"Today," she answered, "nothing."

"Nothing? That's no good," I replied. "Let's see, it's 10:30 here in L.A. so it's lunchtime where you are, what'd you have for lunch?"

"Uh, nothing?"

"Theresa, I can't believe you," I shouted. "It's after 12:30 in the afternoon, what have you eaten today?"

"A diet Coke," she replied. "Richard, you just don't know. I've got four kids to get up and out of the house to school every day. Then I have to get myself dressed and go off to work! Who has time for breakfast?"

"Hey, wait a minute," I came back, "you want to talk about time? My phone starts ringing before I get up in the morning. I've got six dalmatians that have to be fed and taken out for their morning walk and a lot of times I've got a bowl of cereal in one hand and a glass of juice in the other. You've got to *make* the time. Breakfast is the most important meal of the day—you really can't afford to skip it! Now let's pretend I hadn't called you today. Would you have had lunch?"

"Oh yeah, of course I would."

"Okay, and what had you planned to have for lunch today?" I asked her.

"Well . . . I probably would've run over to the McDonald's across the street from work and had a hamburger or a cheeseburger or something."

"Yeah . . . and french fries and maybe a shake, huh?"

"I didn't know you could read minds on top of everything else," she said.

"A lot of the big hamburger chains have low-cal

items on the menu these days," I told Theresa, "you could just as easily have a green salad at McDonald's, and they even give you those cute little packages of dressing with it. Theresa . . . you don't have an excuse for eating this way!"

"You're right again, Richard, but I guess it boils down to a question of convenience."

"Listen to yourself, honey . . . no time in the morning . . . more convenience in the afternoon . . . meanwhile what's happening to Theresa's body? We've laid out a starting meal plan for you. I want you to get started on it right away . . . beginning with lunch this afternoon, is that a deal?"

"I hear you, Richard, thanks for the 'wake up call!' "

"Don't thank me yet," I told her. "You haven't heard the last of me. I'm going to be calling you back soon!"

Click.

Theresa didn't know that when I said I'll call back soon, that I would be calling the very next day! But I was dying to know what she ended up having for lunch.

I had gotten her work schedule so I knew when she got home. Her son answered the phone and I asked for Theresa. "Can you hold on for a minute, she just got back from the grocery store. I hear her coming in now," he told me. Theresa answered the phone and she *was* surprised that I had called back so fast. Before I got to the all-important question about lunch, I couldn't resist being a little nosy and ask, "So, what'd you buy at the supermarket?"

"Let's see, I bought lettuce, tomatoes, radishes, carrots, and a couple bottles of fat free dressing. I'm making myself a big green salad for dinner!"

NEVER GIVE UP

"Hey, sounds like somebody's eating a whole lot better today," I said. "And what about after we talked yesterday, what'd you have for lunch?"

"Would you believe a grilled chicken salad with fat free ranch dressing," Theresa told me, "Oh, and a glass of water!"

I started to give her a big pat on the back but she stopped me, she had more to say, "You know what else, Richard, even though it's only been barely twenty-four hours and I know I probably haven't lost a thing! But I honestly do feel better already. I feel like I'm going in the right direction!"

"There you go, Theresa. And you know, you're absolutely right," I told her. "Now I want you to hold on to that feeling. That's what's going to help you make it all the way to your goal. Whenever you get a little down, I want you to think about our first phone call, it'll make you giggle."

"Thank you, Richard," she said, "and don't worry, I really am going to make it. I know that."

"And I know it, too, Theresa. Let me know how you're doing, okay?"

"Okay, Richard!"

Click.

I will be **patient with myself** and will not become **compulsive** and **obsessed** with losing weight and exercising.

◆

If I didn't do great yesterday, I will try **harder** today.

◆

I will take a **daily inventory** and be **truthful** with myself.

◆

SMALLER OUTSIDE; BIGGER INSIDE

Jonathan's Story

*H*ey look, here comes Big Jonathan! Hey, Jonathan, don't sit on this side of the bus, you may tip it over!"

The other kids laughed as Jonathan boarded the bus parked in front of his elementary school. School was out, it was time to go home and he really wasn't in the mood to be made fun of. Oh, he was used to it by now but that never made it any easier.

Jonathan took his usual seat on the bus and tried to ignore the other kids but a couple of them insisted on giving him a tough time.

"We told you not to sit on this side, Jonathan," one of the kids said, then pushed him.

"Cut it out you guys, stop picking on me!" Jonathan shouted.

"And what if we don't, what are you gonna do,

sit on us?!" Another kid pushed Jonathan again, then another. What had started out as a bunch of kids just horsing around quickly got out of hand. Three of them jumped on Jonathan all at once, leaving him badly bruised and in tears with no one to defend him.

The bus stopped in front of his house and Jonathan gladly got off as the kids who beat him up continued to make fun of him! "You're a crybaby, too, Jonathan, a big, *fat* crybaby!"

"Jonathan, is that you?" It was his mom, Ernie, calling to him from another room of the house as he walked in. "Jonathan," she called again.

Ernie walked into Jonathan's room to find her son crying and covered with red marks from being beaten up by his classmates.

"Jonathan, what's wrong, who did this to you?" Ernie could see that his injuries were severe enough that he would need medical attention. She and her husband, Don, rushed Jonathan off to the nearest emergency room.

The doctor was able to treat Jonathan's injuries just fine. But those were the injuries you could see. There were some other injuries that his parents couldn't see, not right away. From that day on, he was a totally different nine-year-old. He was always "chubby" growing up, but he still was able to do all the things other kids his age could do. He had friends, played outside, rode his bike, but he was different now. Jonathan refused to leave the house. He stuck to his mother like Velcro. He didn't talk as much: he became a loner. Add scared, frightened and insecure as Jonathan went into almost total hibernation.

As his personality changed so did his appetite. Now that he spent so much time indoors, Jonathan made eating the only activity he pursued. Sandwiches, sugary sodas, ice cream, they would never call him names—"We'll be your friends, Jonathan. You don't need those mean old kids at school anyway."

Don and Ernie felt helpless, they sought help at school, with a family counselor, nothing seemed to work. Jonathan was not, and they were beginning to think, was never going to be, the same happy child he was before. His overeating didn't stop, his reclusiveness didn't stop but his weight was going up, ten years old and he was already 163 pounds!

Ernie took the changes in her son very personally, as a mother she felt helpless, even guilty but what else could she do to help him? Each night after dinner, Dan would go watch TV, Jonathan, his sister, Stephanie, and brother, Daniel, would retreat to their rooms and Ernie hoped for a way to bring the happiness back to her home.

Ernie was watching "Good Morning America" when she saw the promo for an appearance I was making on another television show. "Richard Simmons will be on with us this morning at nine. He'll be talking about overweight kids and what you can do to help one. Join us right after GMA!"

A glimmer, Ernie saw just a glimmer of hope. "This I've got to watch," she told herself. But before she sat down to watch the show, Ernie set the VCR. She wanted Jonathan to see the show, too, when he got home from school.

She listened intently as I shared my own experiences as a fat kid back in New Orleans. "I know what it's like to be eleven-years-old and the fattest kid in school. Not only was I the one kid who knew he wouldn't be picked to play when they were choosing sides for the baseball team, but on top of that, I had

NEVER GIVE UP

to deal with 'Moose'! Oh, every school has a Moose, and ours didn't like me at all!

'Hey, Milton,' that was my name back then, 'Hey Milton, you wanna play baseball? Oh, I forgot, you're too fat and clumsy, guess I'll just have to play ball with your head.' I'd take off running and, of course, he would catch me, any kid in school could, then *crack*, he'd whop me over the head with the bat! And that was not just one day but almost every day after school at three o'clock, that's what I had to look forward to. And what did I do after that? Well, I'd eat even more, the food would at least numb the pain in my head. To this day at 3:00 in the afternoon, I automatically want to eat something!"

Not only was Ernie touched by the similarity of my story to Jonathan's, but she found herself traveling back in time to her own childhood. It was like something lodged in her memory had been pried loose and brought back clearly almost thirty years later. Ernie was also a chubby kid and she remembered abuse she had suffered because of it. That was something she could deal with later but right now she just hoped Jonathan would be willing to watch the tape. Maybe this will help, she thought.

Jonathan did want to watch, he and Ernie watched the show together. They sat quietly through my interview and when it was over, he looked at his mother and said, "I want to meet him!"

That was great, Ernie thought, but how am I going to arrange a meeting between Jonathan and Richard Simmons! So she thought she would do the next best thing and get a copy of my program for him later.

When Don got in from work that evening, she told him about the show and her plans to get Jonathan on my program. Later that evening, the family decided to make a shopping trip over to Crystal Mall near their home. They were hopping from store to store when Ernie noticed a sign that for her was nothing less than a sign from Heaven! "Jonathan, Don, look at this . . . can you believe this . . . Richard Simmons is going to be here at the mall next week! This is just too much. We just watched him on TV today . . . we've got to come out and see him!"

Don agreed and they made plans to be at the mall that next Thursday evening. Don even took the day off from work, they wanted to beat the crowd by arriving as early as possible.

The whole family watched and listened while I talked to the audience and worked out with them. Jonathan wanted to come up on stage when I called for all the children in the audience to join me. But he was too afraid, worried that some of his classmates might be there to make fun of him either then or in school the next day.

I ended my appearance by telling the audience: "Overweight people are no different than anyone else. If you think less of someone because of their size, if you make fun of someone because he or she is fat, then you are wrong. We all share the same feelings, the same hopes and dreams, the fact that we are all different in appearance will never change that!"

Jonathan stood next to his parents in tears. I really wish I could meet him and talk with him, he thought to himself.

The show ended and the crowd began to break up. With all the confusion, Jonathan and Ernie got separated from Don and their other two children. As they attempted to regroup, Ernie saw me walking toward the exit with a large group of other people in

NEVER GIVE UP

tow, including mall staffers as well as some people from the audience asking me questions on the way out. Ernie saw a break, but she didn't want to appear rude so she simply shouted to me, "Richard . . . Richard! Please, help me save my son's life!"

I looked over to see Jonathan and his mother, I had so many people talking to me at once. I shouted back to her, "Work hard! You gotta work hard!" I tried to say more but the crowd was literally *carrying* me out of the mall! Ernie and Jonathan managed to relocate the rest of the family and on the drive home, they had a family discussion.

"You know, Don, you and I could stand to lose some weight ourselves. I think the three of us should 'work hard' together. We've always done everything as a family. Why should this be any different?"

Don couldn't agree more, "What do you think of the idea, Jonathan," he asked, "you want your mom and I to do this with you?"

"Sure," Jonathan replied, "I think it's a very good idea."

To prove they meant business, when they got home Ernie started their program by throwing out all the Easter candy they'd bought for the upcoming holiday. After their Deal-A-Meal arrived, they made a trip to the supermarket and brought the food program along with them to use as a grocery "buying guide." They bought extra fruits and vegetables, fish, poultry, rice cakes, low-fat mayonnaise, all the things they would need for a new way of eating.

Ernie found a new use for the clipboard she kept in the kitchen. She took a marker and drew a series of lines across and then down the board. There was a section for Don, one for Jonathan and one for herself. There was a breakfast section, lunch section and, of course, one for dinner. She had created a giant-sized Deal-A-Meal wallet so each day they could all keep track of what they had eaten!

She cooked nutritious low calorie dinners and they all were surprised that after a meal they weren't hungry! They were eating less but felt more satisfied because they knew the family was eating better! Ernie even made enough so that some days they could have leftovers to take to school and to work for lunch the next day! And they discovered . . . exercise!

The living room, where they had all spent night after night lounging around being couch potatoes, was reinvented. Don and Ernie took two of the recliners out of the room all together. Now they had more space to work out. Instead of reclining every night . . . now the whole family exercised to my video tapes. The living room became their personal health club!

His mom and dad were losing weight right along with him and Jonathan was becoming a whole new kid in a hundred ways. He had gotten so fat that he couldn't bend to tie his shoes, Ernie had to do it for him, but not anymore! And that's nothing!

Because he had lost fifty-two pounds, Jonathan had become a regular pro at sports! When his gym class played soccer, he used to kick the ball just anywhere, especially *away* from him. But now when the ball rolled his way, he'd run toward it, kick it and score! (Atta boy, Jonathan!)

He also decided it was time for a new look! Jonathan told Don and Ernie that he wanted new clothes, a new haircut and new glasses. They were happy to whip out the charge cards for him, Jonathan was back and his parents were glad to have him!

The three of them wrote me letters to say how well

NEVER GIVE UP

they were *all* doing but I wanted details . . . so I called! Don answered the phone, he sounded like a kid himself. He told me, "Ernie and Jonathan have gone through a mental and physical transformation and it's the best thing that ever happened to my family."

"Well, what about you," I asked him, "What has changed about Don?"

"For one thing I've lost twenty-nine pounds, Ernie's lost forty-one by the way, but you know I started the program to support Jonathan . . . I had no idea how it would benefit me!"

"Tell me *how* it's helped you, Don."

"Job performance," he answered, "I'll bet you my work has improved a hundred and fifty percent! I just have so much more energy these days!"

Ernie was standing by and was getting impatient with Don because she wanted a chance to brag about her family! She told me how much her son had changed, he was getting better grades in school, his teachers and classmates were in awe of him and he even became best friends with one of the boys who beat him up. "Richard," she said, "You told me at the mall to 'work hard,' well that's exactly what we did and it's paid off better than I could ever have dreamed! Thank you, Richard!"

"For what?" I said. "It was you all that did all the work. I'm very proud for all of you, but where's the star pupil . . . I want to talk to Jonathan!"

"Oh, he's right here," Ernie said, "and he can't wait to talk with you!"

When Jonathan came on, I asked him how it felt to have lost so much weight, fifty-two pounds was a lot of weight for an eleven-year-old boy to lose.

"I'm not shy anymore for one thing," he told me.

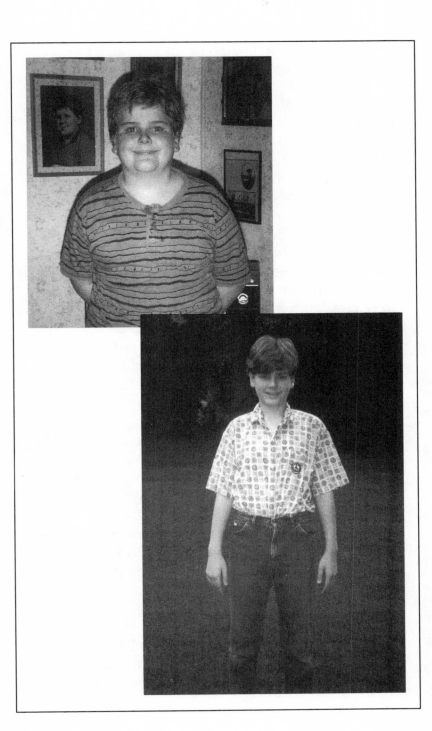

"I'm not afraid of gym class anymore either. I'm even going to soccer camp this summer so I can score even *more* goals next year!"

"And what about your eating habits, Jonathan. What have you learned from this?" I asked. "Do you ever think you'll want to eat the way you used to again?"

"Richard, if I did that, I'd be back where I was in fourth and fifth grades, and I was another person then. I don't ever want to be that person again!"

When I asked Jonathan how it made him feel after the kids on the bus beat him up, his tone changed.

"They made me feel very low, like I was a nobody. Why did they have to do that to me and not somebody else?"

I told Jonathan they were wrong to pick him out for their meanness but they would have been wrong to treat *anybody* that way. Then I asked him the most important question. "Have you forgiven those kids for what they did?"

His answer was, "No."

"Jonathan," I explained, "you've done an incredible job of healing your body but forgiving people for mistreating you is part of the healing. Do you have one of my Project Me Passports?" I asked.

"Yeah."

"Okay, I'm going to read you number five now and when we finish talking I want you to go read it again and again if you have to. But right now I just want you to listen, all right?"

"Okay."

"Number five . . . I forgive those who have made fun of me, judged me or put me down because of my weight." Jonathan was silent. "I could add 'beat me up' to that sentence, Jonathan. You're only eleven-years-old, if you don't learn to forgive people for mistreating you now, how are you going to know how to forgive when you're twenty or thirty years old, huh?"

"But it's so hard, Richard."

"I know it is, Jonathan, but you've proven what a strong young man you are, you can do it . . . I did! Those kids can't call you 'Big Jonathan' anymore but I'm going to ask you to be 'Big Jonathan' one more time . . . I want you to be big enough to forgive!"

MY CLOSET DOESN'T FIT ME ANYMORE.

Pins, alterations, emergency stitches
Knotted elastic and last minute switches,
Handfuls of fabric that's no longer needed
Since much of my girth has so greatly receded.
Billowing shirts and jeans that are saggy,
T-shirts so big they are totally baggy,
I'm proud to announce that from cotton to knits
My closet has nothing within it that fits.

To stand in these clothes that used to be tight
And to feel them so roomy is such a delight.
I can feel my achievement in every loose fold,
The results of changed habits are clear to behold.
For all of those times that I made the right choice
I can see the rewards in these clothes and rejoice.
The following fact simply thrills me to bits
My closet has nothing within it that fits.

It's time to go shopping for regular sizes.
I shall even close zippers with no mean surprises,
Belts will fasten with inches to spare,
Selections so broad there's a chance to compare
Sweaters and underwear, bathing suits, too.
I'm seeing all clothes from a new point of view,
Checking the mall is no longer the pits.
My closet will soon contain something that fits.

I don't want to buy till I've checked every store;
Most I have not ever been in before.
Now I can enter with confidence sure,
No longer those comments or stares to endure.
I feel even lighter, I'm walking on air;
You couldn't imagine unless you've been there.
I shall shop all departments from Saks to the Ritz
And my closet will soon have new clothing that fits!

July 27, 1992

RICHARD SIMMONS' NEVER GIVE UP

JOB'S SISTER

Rosemarie's Story

*T*he longest letter I've ever received was from a woman who had no weight to lose. Diane's best friend, Rosemarie, weighed nearly 1,000 pounds! In fifty handwritten pages, Diane told me Roe's story.

It's the story of a young, chubby Italian girl whose grandmother would get upset if Roe didn't have second helpings of lasagna. And it wasn't long before Grandma didn't have to insist anymore. Little Roe learned to help herself to as much as she wanted.

In school, if she failed a test and needed some cheering up, a few ice-cream cones would usually do the trick. If anyone made fun of her because of the weight, some pizza, some sandwiches or a bag full of Oreos would chase the blues away.

After high school, Roe got married but her new

husband never knew that his wife was already having a secret love affair, with food.

When she prepared her famous meatball and spaghetti dinner, she would make several extra meatballs for herself and eat them long before dinner was put on the table. While he was asleep, she would sneak to the kitchen for a little midnight snack.

Up to this point, Roe had eaten, first as a kind of reward, then as a way to cope with any disappointment in her life. But when I turned another page in Diane's letter, I relived the first major tragedy in Roe's life. And tragedy would soon become a major part of Roe's love affair with food.

Her husband, Richard, had come home from a hunting trip and was sitting in the living room, cleaning his gun. Roe was there with him when the gun accidentally went off, taking his life. I don't know about you, but just the thought of this scene in Roe's life breaks my heart.

With the loss of her husband, Roe's attachment to food grew even stronger. When she got depressed over losing him, she would go so far as to send herself "candy grams" to cheer up.

When her father died of cancer, Roe rang up thousands of dollars in credit card debt on gourmet foods to hide from the realities of her life.

At 600 pounds, Roe ran out of places to hide. She had become so large that she couldn't go out in public without being the center of uninvited attention. She could feel the eyes on her and imagine the comments being whispered behind her back. The final blow came when she was picking up some takeout at her favorite deli and someone asked if she was the fat lady at the circus.

That was it, Roe decided it was time to shut herself

off from the stares and wisecracks forever. In the future her eating and her life would be spent inside the cozy, secure world of home.

The new setup was perfect, instead of going out to get something to eat, she would have the food delivered to her. Without the stimulation of even a simple trip to the supermarket, Roe's life got smaller as she got larger. Roe was gaining weight faster than ever. All physical activity had stopped except for the energy it required to lift a fork to her mouth.

As the weight increased, Roe's health deteriorated. It was getting more and more difficult to take care of herself. Her mother had promised to come out and help her around the house but that visit never happened. Her mother died from a heart attack and yet again Roe had someone special snatched from her life.

Because she was too large to fit in a pew, she had to sit outside on a bench and listen to her mother's eulogy through the open doors of the church. After the service, Roe retreated even further into a private world. And it was a very lonely world. The difficulty in taking care of herself and her deteriorating health forced Roe to spend most of the time in bed. From her bed, she prayed to the Virgin Mary to take her away, too!

Diane's letter ended with a plea of help and guidance for a friend. I reread parts of her letter many times over, walking in Roe's shoes through Diane's words.

I dialed the number to talk to Roe and heard a voice so sad, so lifeless. We talked for over an hour as she told me of the sorrow and the hurt she felt, having very little will left to live.

In my happiest "Broadway voice" I said, "Roe, you have so many things to live for, one of them being

NEVER GIVE UP

Diane's friendship!" I told her to please hang in there and I would call her back tomorrow after I had time to figure out a plan for us.

Diane was there at the bedside when I called and I thanked her for writing me about Roe. It took a lot of love and concern to do what she did, to put someone's soul down on paper.

That same evening, I contacted a doctor friend of mine in Albion, Michigan, who specializes in helping the morbidly obese. We got Roe to the hospital where he practiced and he discovered she had developed an enlarged heart, diabetes and an array of other medical problems.

Doctor Jim explained that he would perform what's called a "gastric exclusion" whereby the size of her stomach would be reshaped to hold smaller amounts of food. It would be a complicated operation but without it, Roe would very likely die.

The day of the operation, I anxiously awaited a phone call from the doctor to let me know how Roe did. He called with the good news I had prayed for . . . "Richard, Rosemarie did great! The surgery was successful and I think this lady is going to make it!"

I called Roe daily to keep up with her recovery. With each conversation I could hear her determination to live grow stronger. When she was well enough to return home, I took a trip to Pleasant Valley, New York, to meet my new friend for the first time.

Roe was sitting in her home outside the bedroom door beneath a sign she had made. It read, WELCOME ST. RICHARD, I LOVE YOU. She had the face of an angel with the eyes of a child. I also got to meet her good friend, Diane, as well as a host of neighbors and friends who had also shown up to celebrate her homecoming. Roe had already lost 200 pounds because of the surgery and was starting to feel like a "real" person again!

After losing 300 pounds, she was able to wash her own car and shovel the snow from her driveway. I've got the pictures to prove it!

After losing 400 pounds, Roe got a job at a deli making sandwiches. It was the same deli that had delivered food to her bedside when she still weighed 980 pounds. And no, she wasn't tempted by those deli sandwiches because the weight loss was more important than pastrami.

Still weighing almost 600 pounds, Roe liked the fact that she was able to hold a job again but she wanted more from life than taking sandwich orders. So she went job hunting all over town but because of the weight, no one would hire her.

One organization saw through her physical appearance though, they saw a woman with a genuine desire to help others. She got a job with the Dutchess County Association for Retarded Citizens, or the ARC it's called for short.

The ARC provides employment opportunities for adults with various types and levels of physical or mental challenges. Her first day on the job, Roe walked into the room and met her 200 co-workers. None of them saw her fat, they could only feel her kindness. At long last, she felt the acceptance that had been missing from her life for so many years.

Starting out on the assembly line where workers assemble products to sell to support themselves, Roe swiftly moved through the ranks to receptionist and from there to floor supervisor. Today, as an ADL spe-

NEVER GIVE UP

cialist (Activities for Daily Living), she is responsible for assisting fourteen adults who live in the ARC residences.

Lots of good things were happening in Roe's life besides excelling in a new job. She was staying on the food program and still losing weight, lots of it! Every time she reached a new milestone, she would send me photos to document the new page in her life. The transformation was a beautiful thing to watch! Most people would not be terribly happy weighing 240 pounds but for where Roe had come from, she felt just like Cinderella must have at the ball!

Every year I've made it a point to get Roe back to Michigan so Dr. Jim could give her a physical. Like clockwork she would return to Albion, get checked out and get the good news: she was doing fine!

When I called to check up on her after the most recent visit, I found out her string of good fortune had been broken, Roe had developed cancer of the uterus.

Dr. Jim gave her a 50/50 chance at best of beating the disease. But even though her chances were only even at winning, Roe kept her spirits up, never slowing down long enough to worry.

In between her visits to the hospital for radiation therapy, she continued to go to work every day to help her group of residents at the ARC. On one of her last drives to work, Roe's car was struck by another woman's who had run a red light! Diane called to tell me what happened and I found myself once again traveling to Pleasant Valley to see my friend.

When I arrived at the house, there was my Roe with a broken collar bone, a fractured rib, a concussion and bruised from head to toe. But instead of lying down, she was standing in the kitchen, supported by a cane. Roe had spent enough time in bed. Now not even a serious car accident could force her to retreat to the bedroom where she had been captive for so many years!

I told her to sit down at the kitchen table to rest so we could talk. "Why me?" she asked, "why is all this happening to me?"

I answered, "Because you're Job's sister."

She looked at me seemingly puzzled, "Job's sister, who's Job?"

Job was a man whose story I read in the Bible. He had many children and many worldly riches and he served God well. Satan told God that the reason Job served Him so well was that he'd been blessed with so many gifts. Satan insisted that if Job's worldly possessions were taken away, then he would turn his back to God. To prove his point, Satan took away all Job's riches, his home, even members of his family. But Job stood fast, never giving up his faith and when Satan saw that he had lost, God restored to Job everything that had been taken away and more!

I said to Roe, "You have the patience and the strength of Job. You've been tested so many times and you always come right back on top!" I told her to get rested up so she could get better because a lot of people depended on her now.

As I pulled away from the house, I saw Roe standing there in the doorway and knowing I couldn't hear her, she mouthed the words, "I love you!"

Back home, I read the story of Job again in the Old Testament to see if I had remembered it correctly. I couldn't wait to call Roe back with a very important addition to the story: Job lived to be 140!

NEVER GIVE UP

I DREAM OF DEBBIE

Debbie's Story

I had never seen Debbie so excited! Don't get me wrong, she was excited after losing 120 pounds with my program and attending my exercise studio. I saw her excited again when she got to appear on one of my Sweatin' videos. But the look on her face when she stopped me in the parking lot after class that evening, well I figured she must have just won the California Lottery!

"Richard . . . Richard, guess what, I'm getting a belly button!" she shouted.

Now, I'm thinking, a belly button, doesn't she already have one, doesn't everybody? I checked to make sure mine was still there; it was!

Debbie explained, "Well, I do have a belly button but I've never been happy with it. Ever since I can remember, mine was lost in those folds of fat you get when you're overweight, so it's like it was never there. And now that I've lost weight, I've found myself a good plastic surgeon and he's gonna give me a brand new belly button. Wish me luck!"

The very next day Debbie went to see the doctor for her consultation. Later on, she told me all about the visit. She was instructed to undress down to her underwear and be ready to pose for a few Polaroids. A nurse came in with a camera, introduced herself and said, "Okay Debbie, turn to the side, please," and Click. She heard the first snapshot come rolling out of the camera. The nurse continued, "All right, now face me, honey," and Click. She got a frontal view. Debbie kept right on smiling until the nurse was finished.

"Now, I know how those models at *Playboy* must feel," she said.

The doctor came in. He examined Debbie's photos quietly, looked her over again and declared her the perfect candidate for this surgery. Then he asked her just what kind of belly button she would prefer! "Would you like an 'inny' or an 'outy?' " he said. "Don't answer me yet! You like to shop, don't you?"

"Me? Oh my yes," Debbie replied, "I *love* to shop!"

With that, the doctor reached into a cabinet and pulled out a huge photo album. It contained pictures of people who'd already had the surgery along with illustrations of various types of belly buttons. He instructed her, "Now take your time going through the catalogue until you find one you like."

Debbie flipped through the pages with great care, not wanting to miss a single one; hey, this was an important decision! When one photo in particular stood out, she stopped. "Here, right here . . . this one," she exclaimed, pointing the photo out for the doctor. "I want this one, it looks just like Cher's!"

With the selection made, a date was set for surgery.

As the big day rapidly approached, Debbie began to consider just how serious a procedure she was about to undertake. A cold wind seemed to be blowing across her feet. She began asking herself all sorts of questions: what if something goes wrong like I don't come out from the anesthesia, who'll make sure my kids go to college? Or what if the doctor makes a mistake and my belly button ends up in some strange place, like on my side or something? Do I really want to go through with this?!"

Continuing to roll all the questions around inside her head, Debbie was worrying herself to near mania! She dropped out of exercise class, started overeating again and put on seven pounds. She was actually starting to feel sick and decided to make an appointment to see her regular physician before going through with the tummy surgery.

She admitted to him that her nerves had gotten so bad she couldn't exercise anymore, all she could do was eat. The doctor ran a number of tests and when he was done, had a little chat with Debbie. "It appears that your problem is stress, plain and simple, probably over this operation you're about to have. It would be best if you put it off for a while, calm yourself down and get back to normal."

That was fine with Debbie but she had a question, "Well, aren't you going to give me something for my nerves in the meantime?"

The doctor's answer was a resounding, "No. What I want *you* to do is get back to your exercise and diet plan. That's *exactly* what you need right now!"

We were all happy to see her back in class. She had been missing from action for over a month but got back "into the groove" quite smoothly. Returning

NEVER GIVE UP

to the program was what the doctor had ordered and Debbie could not have been given better advice! She got her confidence back, dropped the few pounds she'd gained and reached the conclusion to go ahead with the surgery. "It's now or never!" she said.

The patient arrived at the hospital right on schedule at 5:30 A.M. Debbie had no idea she was already a minor celebrity before getting to the hospital. Some of the nurses had heard about her weight loss, her appearance in my exercise video and knew she attended my studio. They came into her room all excited, each with what seemed like a hundred questions to ask! "How'd you lose the weight? How do you keep it off? Is Richard Simmons really as crazy in person as he is on TV?"

Their visit was cut short when it was time for Debbie to leave for the operating room. As an intern rolled her down the hallway, she couldn't figure out what, but something was wrong with this picture. "Excuse me," she asked the accompanying nurse, "but aren't I supposed to be knocked out for this little operation?"

Apparently during the earlier hubbub in her room, someone had forgotten to have the anesthesia administered. The intern promptly made a U-turn back to the room and Debbie was sent off to dreamland.

And that's all she remembers until waking up hours later alone in her hospital room. Oh my . . . I did it, I really did it . . . I just hope it turned out okay, she wondered, still rather groggy. She didn't have to wait to find out. The doctor came in to tell her what a good patient she'd been, "And now you'll just have to be patient a little longer."

A few days later it was time for the unveiling. Debbie felt like she was in a scene from *The Invisible Man* as the bandages were carefully snipped away. "Take a look," the doctor said, "now you're a little swollen but I think you will be very proud."

Still feeling sore, Debbie raised her head just enough to look down, see her stomach and exclaim, "Oh my God . . . it's flat! And there's a hole there and it's where it's supposed to be! I got my belly button!"

And now that she does, Debbie's one happy lady! Already a natural born shopper, she no longer has to limit the styles of clothes she buys. On a recent shopping trip with her daughter, she couldn't resist trying on a little two-piece number she saw in a boutique's window. The blouse was one of those "crop tops" that shows off the tummy.

She took the ensemble into a dressing room, slipped it on and after studying herself in the mirror called her daughter in for a second opinion. "What do you think, Ansley, do I look okay in this?" Of course she already knew the answer, Madonna couldn't have looked any better in it!

After a complete recovery, Debbie returned to class. One evening after class she proudly lifted her top just enough to show off her proudest new possession, "Well, Richard, how does it look?"

I've got to tell you, the only thing missing was a little jewel in the center and she would have been ready for belly dancing lessons!

Some may call it vanity, but I call it a well-earned reward for a woman who worked extra hard to achieve her goal. If there's something in *your* life that you can't "stomach," remember Debbie!

NEVER GIVE UP

THE CANDYMAN CAN

Jason's Story

*J*ason's pictures slipped out of the letter he wrote me and for a moment, I thought they were snapshots of me when I was fifteen-years-old. Frankly, I had a difficult time reading his biography because it was parallel to my own story in so many ways.

Jason had been fat his entire life. The same excuses I used for my weight problem, he used for his. Excuses like, "I have big bones, I have a glandular problem or my mom is fat so that's why I'm fat."

Like me, Jason also became the class clown, laughing with the other kids when they smashed cupcakes in his face and having them use him for a punching bag after school.

On many a morning, he would hold his arms across his face then press so hard that his face turned beet red. Then he would pretend to be sick and try to get out of going to school. Other days he would become so disgusted with his appearance, he'd literally beat himself up!

Jason hated shopping for clothes, not only was it not fun but he hated having to always go to the "husky" department or to "big men" shops to find those size 54 jeans he was currently wearing. He spent a lot of time just sitting in his room daydreaming about how it would feel to be a "regular" size teenager and look like everybody else.

I finished reading the last line of his letter and called him at home right away. His mom, Linda, answered the phone. He was in his room asleep but she was happy to run and wake him up. As I waited for him to get to the phone, I flipped through the photos again.

One picture showed Jason sitting on a couch opening Christmas gifts and not looking particularly happy. Another was of him sitting in a lawn chair on the deck, wearing shorts and a T-shirt that barely covered his 300 pounds. Before I could examine another photo, I heard his voice over the phone.

"Richard . . . is this really you? You got my letter, this isn't a joke or anything is it?"

I assured Jason that no one was playing a joke on him: "Well of course it's me, Jason, and I really want to help you." I immediately went into my "interview mode" finding out what his favorite foods were, what he ate at school, how much exercise he got, those kind of questions. After just five minutes of talking, I could see Jason didn't have very much knowledge of nutrition. When I was his same age, I'd never really heard of the word *nutrition* and most probably would have lost a spelling bee if it came up!

I told him I'd like to be his friend and teacher and

promised to write him soon. Before our conversation ended, I said, "I believe you can do this! Picture yourself the way you want to look, close your eyes and see what you look like without that extra weight. I want you to think about the 'new you' every day!"

I was sitting in my office during that call and my personal Deal-A-Meal wallet was lying on my desk next to his photos. I decided to pack it up and send it on to Jason.

I waited to see if he would write again. It was important for me to give him time to think about his own commitment to weight loss. He did and we became constant pen pals. He would send me cartoons he'd drawn, some were self-portraits. There were slogans written all over the pages like, THINK THIN, YOU'LL WIN! IT'S AS EASY AS PIE! But the word *pie* would be scratched out and the word *broccoli* substituted. (There's another word I would have missed at the spelling bee, that vegetable was *never* allowed on my plate!)

More letters followed with "weight updates." Jason started educating himself about food, he was learning to think before he would eat. In one letter he wrote me, "I'm sticking to 1,600 calories a day with no problem. I used to have a daily ritual of eating at least one large candy bar. Out of curiosity I looked at the wrapper to see how many calories it had and I was shocked, 550 calories! That's one third of what I'm eating now for a whole day! I decided it just wasn't worth it!" After reading that, I knew Jason was becoming "food smart!"

During one of our phone chats, I told Jason I had a real surprise for him. I travel nearly 300 days out of the year and my favorite reason for getting out on the road is to appear at shopping malls. We go in,

NEVER GIVE UP

build a huge stage, put in a killer sound system and hold a giant Sweatin' To The Oldies class for all the shoppers to come out to see me.

"And guess what," I said to Jason, "one of my next stops is your hometown, Tacoma, Washington! I've seen your before pictures and now that you've lost sixty-five pounds, I'd like to see your after pictures, live and in person. Will you come out to visit me?"

It was a Saturday afternoon and the Tacoma Mall was packed! I was so afraid that Jason would get lost in the sea of faces. I call people up onstage to exercise with me by groups when I do these shows and the next group was to be my teenagers.

The teens started filling up until the stage was filled to capacity. I searched the group for the face of my special guest. I wanted to see if I could recognize him from the photos he'd sent me but apparently his continuing weight loss was making the job more difficult. Or maybe he just didn't show up. That thought was terrible. Before I had a chance to call for him over to the microphone, a young man sneaked up from behind, tapped my shoulder and said, "Hi, do you know who I am?"

Of course, it was Jason and he looked great! We had a blast exercising to a song by his favorite singer, Mariah Carey. After the show was over I told him how different he looked from his original photos. His response was, "Thanks, Richard, but I don't just look different, I am different! I feel good about who I am now!"

Jason sent me an Easter card a couple months later and he'd lost even more weight, there are photos to document his progress. His card was so funny, it had pictures of Baby Ruths, Butterfingers and a host of other chocolate bars we would all know, (okay . . .

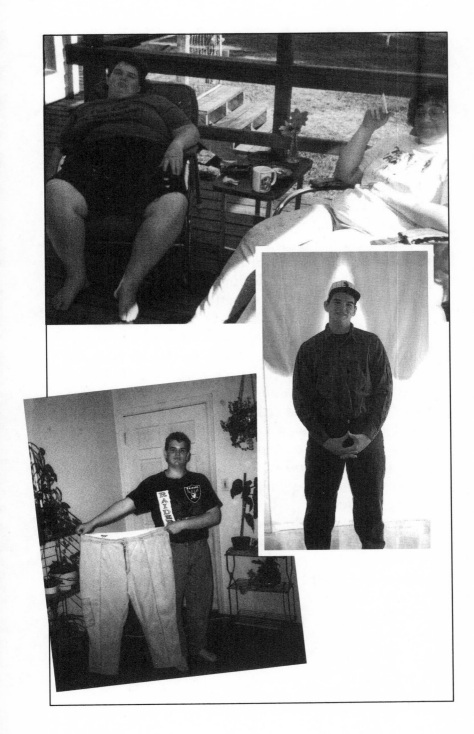

and *love!*). In the top corner of the card was one of those manufacturers coupons good for a free bar for any of them. But Jason had scribbled next to the coupon, "Richard, don't use this!" Well, I didn't, Jason, but I did keep the card.

I asked my young friend recently what has kept him going. He had a great answer, "I was really tired of being embarrassed every summer when everyone else was wearing shorts and stuff. You can imagine how *I* looked wearing them. I faced up and admitted to myself that fat is not where it's at! On days that I got most discouraged, I would just do like you told me and picture myself in the physical state I really wanted to be in. To me, losing weight is like running a race; once you reach a certain point, there's no turning back!"

Out of the mouths of babes . . . Jason's total weight loss is now 114 pounds, he's down to a lean, mean 187! His story is special to me because as kids, we were cut from the same mold. Our playmates were waiting for us on the candy aisle at the corner drugstore! That I was able to be a part of his newfound self-confidence gives more meaning to my own life.

By the way, Jason has a new part-time job. He's working at, and are you ready for this, McDonalds! But he assured me he's not dipping into the Chicken McNuggets while he's working under the golden arches, he has the garden salad instead!

Good for you, Jason! You'll never have to listen again to the other kids' "Snickers" because you look so "Chunky!" You hit "Payday" when you lost that weight and today you look like "100 Grand!"

CHILD'S PLAY

Linda's Story

*W*hen Linda got the pictures back that were taken at Christmas, she was alarmed at how fat her son, Jason, was. She'd always worried about his weight and the photos of him were a jolting reminder of how out of control his eating habits were. Is this my fault? she wondered. Am I to blame, maybe my divorce had something to do with this. Did I raise my son to be fat? In Linda's case, history had sadly repeated itself.

She could remember back to her own childhood, the loud arguments between her parents that eventually resulted in divorce, she was only in fourth grade at the time. For three years after the breakup, she lived with her mother.

She had always been closer to her father and refused to have anything to do with the rules laid down in her mom's house. Exhausted with Linda's rebellion, her mother thought it would be better for her to move in with Dad.

By that time, her father had remarried and Linda couldn't get along with her stepmother either. They fought bitterly and constantly with one of those fights getting so serious, Linda landed in a detention center. While it may sound like she was the original Bad Seed, her real intention was to see her natural parents together again. She just didn't know how to go about accomplishing it.

Fighting with the family was not the only way Linda vented frustration: she also ate. There were very few meals for her in the school cafeteria, she spent her lunch money on candy bars, brownies at the bakery and her favorite, sidewalk sundaes.

No matter how much her father tried she simply couldn't get along with anyone in his home without some kind of conflict. Pretty fed up with the situation herself, Linda dropped out of eleventh grade and moved in with her older sister where she would live and work taking care of her sister's children.

Barely a year later, she met and married a young GI and soon she had four children of her own to take care of. That marriage turned out to be every bit as bumpy as her parents' and also ended in divorce.

Linda hated the idea of being alone and raising four kids by herself. Just two months after the divorce, she was married again and had one more child. It was another turbulent ride and this time the union lasted only two years. Now she had five children to care for and some serious thinking to do.

She could have easily become a "welfare mother," but that wasn't the kind of life she wanted for herself or the kids. Instead, Linda went back to school, got her GED, high school general equivalency diploma, then government grants and put herself through business college. This was an impressive feat in itself but she still didn't feel very special.

As Linda was expanding her mind, she was also expanding her inseam. She built her life around her children and pushed everything else aside. She worked full-time and did a fine job at home raising five kids. And she weighed 245 pounds.

One by one the kids grew up, moved out into the "grown-up" world until Linda was left at home with just her youngest son. After a look back at her own life and now staring at the picture of her 300-pound son, Linda was close to answering her own questions.

She remembered those rough years after the second divorce when her son first started putting on weight. A trip to the doctor with him revealed no medical reason for his weight gain. And she would often catch him in the kitchen, eating cookies or eating from a jar of peanut butter. He was looking for love in a jar of Jif!

Yes, she did raise her son to be fat and chances were the turmoil of divorce may have played a part in his obesity. She couldn't help but notice the unhappy expression on his face in the photos taken on Christmas day when a kid should be at his happiest. But since Linda was doing nothing about her own weight problem, how on earth was she going to be able to help her son?

Now, you're not going to believe this, but while Linda was having these thoughts, Jason wrote me a letter on his own asking for help. Very late one evening, locked away in his room, he wrote the letter that would eventually make him not only lose weight himself, but serve as a catalyst for his mother's new body as well!

Linda was so happy for Jason when he got that first phone call from me. It was like a great burden of responsibility had been taken away. She didn't have the first clue on how she could have helped him and now he had done something to help himself.

She was even happier when Jason announced the loss of his first twenty pounds. Yes, happy for him yet sad for herself because she still wasn't losing the weight. But her son, Jason, had his whole life in front of him, she thought, whereas she shouldn't bother because no one really cared about her.

Jason kept right on losing as I stayed in constant touch, giving that extra nudge! When I invited him to join me at the Tacoma Mall, it was Linda who drove him down to see me.

She and Jason watched with the rest of the crowd as I tried to motivate them as well as make them laugh. When Jason's moment came to shine on stage with me, Linda was full of pride. Her baby had already lost sixty-five pounds and she thought he looked great on stage!

Near the end of my appearance I always try to get really serious and stress to the audience how important it is to eat right, exercise and take care of their bodies and minds. I didn't realize it but Linda was really taking in what I had to say. Even though there were several thousand people there, she felt like I was speaking directly to her. And maybe it was her time to get the message because she left the mall feeling there was a wonderful person inside her body of fat and it was time to set that person free forever!

When they got home from the show she had Jason get his Deal-A-Meal program and show her how it worked. She saw how easy it was to follow and after getting one herself began a real effort to change the

way she looked. How funny life can be! After worrying all that time about Jason's weight, it was Jason leading her down the path to better health!

If she had a question about portions, Jason would have the answer. When he felt like having a partner along for his daily walks, Mom was at his side. The two of them had their goals in sight and would let nothing stop them from getting there. Jason lost 114 pounds and here's the sequel: Linda has lost 50 pounds and is down to 195!

The new pride she's discovered beamed through in a recent letter. "It's like living in a new body, it's wonderful! I actually buy and wear bright colors and pretty things now instead of the dull, boring things I used to put on. I feel like I'm glowing all the time!"

Jason's pretty excited about his mom's new image, too. She got a little confused after coming in from work one day wearing a particularly stunning outfit.

"Wow, Mom! You look really fly!" he said.

Now Linda didn't think saying she looked like a "fly" was the most flattering compliment he could pay her. But Jason quickly explained, "No . . . not like a housefly! I mean like one of the 'Fly Girls' on TV. It means you look really hot!"

Mom and son are still on the program watching those last pounds "fly" away. Needless to say, their weight loss adventures have brought them closer. It's like I always say, "The family that weighs together, stays together!"

I know now there are no **easy ways** to do
this. I know the only way to achieve my
goal is through **exercise, eating healthy**
and **staying motivated.**

◆

I will use my **sense of humor** today for it
heals loneliness, depression, insecurity and
boredom.

◆

This time I am doing this for **me.**

◆

WALKIN' WOMAN

Patricia's Story

*T*he doctor said, "I have never seen such heel spurs in my life!" Patricia was alarmed by the doctor's concern. "I'm surprised you can even walk." As he spoke, the doctor referred to a diagram of a foot. "Take a look at this chart. Your heel spurs are bigger than the biggest ones shown here! You'd better lose some weight or those feet aren't going to last you another year."

Patricia left the doctor's office with prescriptions she couldn't afford and the prospect of surgery she was scared to death of having.

Heel spurs, Patricia thought as she climbed into her little Plymouth. She sat there for a moment just looking at the damage 260 pounds of weight had caused to her feet. The doctor's words echoed in her mind but she forced them away.

Well, I can always get to where I want to go

by just putting this key into the ignition. With that thought, Patricia drove away, thinking nothing more about the doctor or the surgery he talked about. She even dumped the prescriptions when she got home. Her life went on as before, heel spurs and all. She drove to work, drove home, ate dinner, went to bed and did her laundry on Sunday nights.

But there is one particular Sunday night she will never forget because it caused her life to change. Patricia was in her bedroom sorting laundry, watching TV and listening to the rain that had been pouring down all day. The phone rang while she was doing her chores and at first she thought it was the phone from the TV show she was watching so she missed the call. It rang again and she grabbed it only to receive some shocking news.

Her mother was on the phone screaming . . . "Pat, Pat honey . . . Whitey couldn't reach you so she called me! Your car's been stolen!"

Almost dropping the phone, Patricia rushed downstairs in the rain to find her usual parking spot empty! She looked around thinking maybe she had parked in a different spot tonight or maybe even in the excitement of it all she was standing on the wrong street. But her mother had been right. This was her street, this was her parking space and her car really was gone!

Standing there in the pouring rain, all she could do was stare at that empty space while a thousand thoughts ran through her head. She couldn't yet believe the car was really gone. Patricia's best friend and neighbor, Whitey, came outside and joined her. The two of them got into Whitey's car and drove up and down every street in the neighborhood hoping that maybe, just maybe, they would find her car.

After searching late into the night, they finally gave up.

Patricia had very little to tell the police, "Why would anyone want to steal that old piece of junk," she wondered. "That car had over eighty thousand miles on it. I got it at an auto auction. Why me?" She spent the rest of the night asking herself the same questions over and over again.

But none of what happened really sank in until the next morning when she realized she would have to take the bus to work . . . Oh, my God . . . *the bus.* It had been ages since she'd been forced to take public transportation and it seemed to require so much more effort to get to work than just getting in her little Plymouth and driving away.

Getting dressed, walking downstairs and onto the street, she had to pass the place where her car would normally be parked. Patricia boarded the Number 61 bus for Long Island City. All during the trip she could only think of one thing: she was carless . . . and she hated the feeling of being "a woman without wheels."

The number 61 let her off at her stop and at that moment she realized she was still blocks and blocks and blocks away from the office!

She had no choice, she was going to have to walk it. It was time to put one foot in front of the other and get herself to work. Step by step and cursing those car thieves with every step she took, Patricia began the longest walk she had ever taken in her life.

Huffing and puffing, Patricia finally reached the door to her office. Her face was bright red, she was totally out of breath and there wasn't a dry spot on her body. Literally crawling into her office, she took

NEVER GIVE UP

off her shoes and propped up her swollen, aching feet.

Well . . . even with the world's biggest heel spurs, you made it, she thought. Patricia was feeling a certain sense of accomplishment. She had learned to turn her anger into mileage! She realized that even though thieves had her stolen car, they couldn't stop her from doing what she *had to do*!

That morning's walk would be the beginning of many long walks for Patricia. It dawned on her if she could walk to work, then she could walk for her *health*, too. Days of walking turned into weeks, the weeks turned into months and along the way something else happened she was not expecting. The pounds dropped off: seventy-one pounds so far!

Recently, I asked Patricia if she had plans yet to buy a new car. She laughed and told me, "Oh I don't know, Richard, I'll think about it in another fifty pounds!"

A LEAGUE OF HIS OWN

Richard's Story

*I*t was the day after Thanksgiving that I first called Richard. He was very surprised to hear my voice because, he said, frankly, he had given up on hearing from me. A month had passed since he'd written and he had a right to be discouraged. But during the holiday season I usually get such a crush of mail, it takes a little longer to play catch up. I apologized for my tardiness but said, "I'm here for you now."

Richard was a big man, a giant at 6 feet 7 inches and over 500 pounds. He explained that his road through life had been a turbulent one and he was feeling very lost. He was a local boy, lived here in the Los Angeles area and I invited him to attend one of my Project Me Motivational classes.

I alerted my staff to take extra care of Richard. He seemed to be going through a very delicate state emotionally. The Saturday he walked into the lobby of my club, he was greeted by Lisa at the front desk. "Well, hello, you must be Richard, come on in. We're really glad you're here." The little bit of recognition in those few words made a difference. Later he would tell me, he instantly felt at home.

Lisa escorted him to the workout room where he sat with me and a room full of strangers. He listened as our members shared personal success stories and progress reports, felt encouraged every time someone stood to announce their weight loss. He decided right then and there, he was going to be one of those successes, too!

After the motivational meeting was over, as always, I said, "Now get up . . . it's time to exercise!" I could see panic on Richard's face as the rest of the class eagerly got up to start the workout. He hadn't attempted anything remotely close to real exercise in all his twenty-six years!

I like to keep a watchful, almost "parental," eye on our first timers but with Richard, I made sure to watch a bit more carefully. He was obviously having a rough go of it. His face had become very pale and he seemed to have trouble breathing. He was really pushing himself which would be good in the long run, but not a good idea for his very first day. As class continued, I walked over to him, the top of my head barely reaching his chest. Looking up, I said, "Slow down! This is your first time, I want you to do only as much as you can. If you have to take a break and catch your breath, do it! You can always rejoin us later." And Richard did rejoin us: each time he came back to class his breathing and movements improved.

As he became more comfortable with us, he took more of a role in the discussion part of class, he was starting to lose weight. It was time to put him under the spotlight, "Richard, stand up and tell everyone how much you've lost," I told him.

He stood, rising high above the others in the class, "I've been coming to class every day for a month now, I'm staying on the food program and I've lost twenty-four pounds." The whole class began applauding much to Richard's surprise. He couldn't understand why they were making such a big deal out of a lousy twenty-four-pound weight loss. He could barely see a difference in his body and still had so far to go.

Many of you who've lost 100, 200 pounds or more know the scenario. When you have that much weight to lose, those first fifty pounds or so may not be too visible to the naked eye. The important thing is not to get depressed over it, keep going, your new body *will* bloom, just like Richard's was doing.

A couple more months of faithful exercise and watching his eating habits and he'd lost 110 pounds! My friendly giant as I refer to him, became a dedicated disciple. I knew that when I drove up to the studio, his would always be one of the first smiles to greet me.

After class one evening, he asked if I could do him a favor. He wanted me to write a letter about his progress so that he could give it to his probation officer.

Now none of us at the club knew very much about Richard's personal life so I was caught a little off guard. "Probation officer," I said, "You mean like on 'Dragnet'?!" I was right . . . it was just like "Dragnet."

He asked for a few minutes of my time to explain and I told him I was all ears. He told me about his passionate love for baseball. He'd been a Little League and high school umpire until age nineteen when he had to give up his dream career. His increasing weight and the accompanying aches and pains had made the job impossible.

Rather than lose weight, he continued to overeat and gain more weight. When his best friend died of cancer, the unexpected shock only served to worsen his self-indulgence. He turned to cocaine to mask the pain and when that no longer did the job, he started drinking heavily, too!

Every day Richard would go to his job, return home to his kitchen, a bottle of booze and several lines of coke. His social life all but disappeared. In three short years he put on 120 pounds, going from job to job to support his three deadly sins until there were no jobs left. Not a company in L.A. would hire him because of the way he looked.

Now not only could he not have his dream job, he couldn't get a job doing anything at all.

Outcast and out of luck, Richard had maintained one friendship and that was with Dan, his eating and drinking buddy. An owner of two nightclubs, he gave his pal Richard a chance, putting him in charge of all the business transactions and that meant handling all the money.

The new responsibility and stroke of good fortune did nothing to improve his bad habits. Richard's judgment was so clouded by alcohol and substance abuse that suicide had become the only thing he could think about.

In what he recalls as a moment of insanity, he stole $5,000 from the safe at the nightclub. Purchasing a first-class ticket to Florida, Richard checked into a hotel where he spent the entire night snorting a full ounce of cocaine and drinking liquor, hoping he would either pass out or die. He didn't die.

Richard woke up three days later in a strange place frightened and confused. What am I doing, this is crazy! he thought. He had stolen from a trusted friend then tried to kill himself by snorting and drinking himself to death. Realizing he couldn't run anymore, Richard wanted to return home and make things right. A four-day bus ride back to Los Angeles gave him plenty of time to think about how to right the wrongs he had committed.

After turning himself in to the police, he pleaded guilty to grand theft, a felony charge in the state of California. Part of the conditions his judge set for bail were that he attend a drug rehabilitation center and submit to random drug testing. Richard had made his trip to my health club part of his own rehab process. His sentencing date was coming up and he thought a letter from me might help convince the judge that he shouldn't go to jail.

The court date arrived and Richard sat nervously while his attorney pleaded his case. The judge listened quietly and read the documents in front of him including the letter I had written. He looked Richard over long and hard. He had to be thinking how different, how much better he looked since his appearance before the court several months earlier.

His 110-pound weight loss was impressive and the judge congratulated him. He sentenced Richard to three years probation, continued rehab and counseling *and* by order of the court, he *must* continue taking classes at Slimmons!

Richard was so relieved and he had to laugh. He had every intention of continuing drug rehab and

NEVER GIVE UP

certainly wasn't about to give up his classes at the club!

You should see him in class today! You still wouldn't miss him towering above his "co-sweaters!" He was inspired by so many of them on his first visit to the studio but today he's inspiring newcomers with his own 260-pound loss!

He's also working hard outside class to put the pieces of his life back together. Remember his friend, Dan? It took some time but bit by bit he's repaid the $5,000 he'd stolen and in the process rebuilt a friendship.

Remember that dream of being a professional league umpire he'd forfeited? Richard is back on the ball field calling the plays on high school games again. Wait, there's more! Next year he goes to Cocoa Beach, Florida, for professional umpires school!

Just a month ago Richard called me all excited to tell me that the felony charges against him were completely dismissed and the case closed. But I'll never close the door on Richard. When I talk about the value of determination and believing in yourself, his life is a shining example of exactly what I mean. At the bottom of the ninth inning, bases loaded, he slammed the ball out of the park with a true home run!

STAND BY YOUR MAN

Carol's Story

*C*arol was always sort of a skinny kid growing up. That was until she fell in love and got married. Of course, she had to make a good impression on her new husband, Roger, which meant preparing three very large home cooked meals each day. Slowly the weight started coming up. But it really didn't matter because being a good wife was the most important thing in her life.

She and Roger wanted to have a baby but after years of trying they were still unable to conceive. To console herself, Carol ate out of sadness and depression and continued to gain weight.

Six years into their marriage they decided to adopt a baby. They were fortunate enough to be able to adopt a beautiful two-day-old baby boy. They named him Todd.

Carol decided to quit her job, stay home and be

a full-time mother. While she was home with Todd every day, her days were filled with Todd . . . and food. When Todd napped, Carol would be idle. Sometimes she'd eat. As he began to eat real food, just by habit Carol would snack when he did.

As Todd got older and started school, Carol decided to return to work to earn extra money to help her family buy a new home. She felt her life could not be more perfect.

Early one morning while Roger was out scraping ice from his windshield, he felt an agonizing pain in his neck. Being a heavy equipment mechanic, aches and pains were nothing new to him. But Carol decided to play it safe and take him to see the doctor.

After what seemed like countless X rays and other tests, the doctor informed them that Roger had suffered severe damage to his neck from years of strain on the job. The problem would have to be corrected with immediate surgery.

Carol knew her husband was in a great deal of pain and hoped that the operation would relieve it. She was a nervous wreck during his operation, but the surgery was successful and the doctor informed them that everything looked good: Roger was going to be okay.

But a few days after Carol got the good news and while Roger was still in the hospital, a bone slipped from the fusion in his neck and Roger lost all feeling in the left side of his body. He had to go right back into surgery and have it corrected. After extensive physical therapy and rest for the next few months, he was eventually given the okay to return to work.

Roger and Carol had been through more than their share of problems by now but neither were prepared for what would happen next. Barely two months after Roger had returned to his job, he woke up with severe pains, this time in his back. The doctor advised more physical therapy but it did not help take away his pain. Roger ended up back in surgery to repair what turned out to be a ruptured disk.

This time though, the surgery went even less smoothly and due to complications, one surgery turned into three and Roger had to spend thirty-one days in the hospital.

Meanwhile, Carol tried to be as strong as she could. Sometimes she felt torn apart and wished there were two of her. When she wasn't at the hospital helping Roger get better, she was at home seeing to Todd's needs. And when Carol was all alone at night, she cried and comforted herself: with food.

The worst news of all came when Roger's doctor told him that Roger's injuries would make it impossible for him to work again. Roger and Carol were totally unprepared for this news. They had worked so hard to start a family, buy a home and make a good life for themselves.

Now everything changed. It was up to Carol to meet all the family expenses. The salary from her one full-time job was no longer enough. She had to go out and find two part-time jobs as well to keep her family and their home together.

Carol left home each morning at 6:00 and did not return until 10:00 at night. While she worked all day, family and friends would take care of Roger. But when she got home from work, another job awaited her; it would be her turn to take care of him.

If Roger needed medication, she had to get it for him. If he had to get up from the chair, she had to help him up. The hardest part of all though was helping Roger up the stairs to bed at night. She felt as if

NEVER GIVE UP

she were carrying the weight of the whole world on her shoulders.

Every time there had been a new tragedy in Carol's life, she ate. But she didn't pay much attention to what was happening to her body, though she did notice a lot more aches and pains. She finally decided to take a minute for herself and dust off the old bathroom scale. Carol couldn't believe it when the numbers flew past 200 and stopped at 213 pounds. That skinny little kid wasn't skinny anymore!

Now Carol had something else to worry about and reason to do some really serious thinking: "My son needs a mom and my husband needs me to be healthy so I'm able to help him. I can't keep doing this to myself."

She had heard about my Deal-A-Meal weight loss program but with her tight budget saw it as a luxury she couldn't afford. Now a determined Carol decided she would work extra hours on one of her jobs, save enough money to purchase the program and give it a try.

Exactly one year from the day she started Deal-A-Meal, I heard from Carol for the first time. She poured her heart out to me in a letter, describing in great detail all the trauma she and her family had been through. I must say it was all very depressing.

The mood of her letter did a quick about-face though, when I got to the sentence where Carol told me, "I am now sixty-three pounds lighter! I have gone from a size 22 to a size 12 . . . thank you!"

Not only had Carol become the bread winner for the family, now she was the "fat burner," too! This lady had been tested many times over and each time she picked up the ball, ran with it and scored!

When I called to congratulate her, she had even

more good news to share. She had lost five more pounds. Todd, who had also been gaining weight, lost ten pounds. And dear old Roger was down fifteen pounds, too.

Wait, there's more! Roger's job came through with lifetime financial support so Carol is back to working just one full-time job.

Carol feels like she has been reborn. "What a joy it is to be around the two most important men in my life." When I mentioned how I applauded her courage through the hard times she replied, "I stood by them, but the two of them stood by me as well!"

WHERE'S MAMA?

Mary Ann's Story

Dear Richard,

I don't know how to begin this letter and convey my feelings adequately. I started your program last April with a weight of 299 pounds. I was tired of being fat. I wanted to be thin.

My son had left for college in January of that year. I was beginning to look harder at myself and I didn't like what I saw.

One day, I was watching TV and saw your Deal-A-Meal program and decided this could be the thing that could work for me. I ordered it and waited for my program to arrive.

I remember the day it came, my husband just looked at me and you could tell what he was thinking, "Another waste of money!"

On April 4, I started working the evening shift and that was also the day I chose to start my new life. The first week was the hardest and I felt myself start to weaken so I put on your cassette that comes with the program. It was very inspirational and I could feel my commitment strengthen.

When I got your first exercise video, I would play it every morning and when it got to the part where you ask us, "Do you want to do the twist?" I would answer you back, "No!" but I would twist anyway! My daughter would be on the phone with her friend and when she would hold the phone out while I was screaming, "No," she and her friend would giggle at me.

I knew the day would come when my response would be *yes, yes, yes!* Richard, now I enjoy it and look forward to my exercise every day! I have all four of your tapes now and do them daily. I rotate them and I never get bored.

My son, away at college, had no idea I was dieting. I had told my family that they were not to tell him anything at all about me losing weight. In the beginning it was easy for them to keep my secret; I'm sure they figured that in time I would fail! But as the time went on and they saw how well I was doing on the program, they encouraged me, especially my daughter. She would buy me greeting cards congratulating me on my weight loss. My younger son, Andrew, would say, "That's the way to go, Mom!" My husband would look at me with such a wonderful "twinkle" in his eye. It just made everything worthwhile and most of all, I started to respect myself!

On June 12 at 11:35 A.M., my son's plane landed. He was coming home to be married and he hadn't seen me now for seventeen months. And best of all, he didn't have a clue about my "secret." As you can see from the enclosed picture, this was the woman he was looking for to greet him when he got off the plane. But instead, he was greeted by the "new me!"

His fiancée and my daughter drove to the airport with me. I trailed behind them walking through the terminal, wearing my sunglasses. When his plane landed and he got off the plane, my daughter and future daughter-in-law went to hug him. Still wearing my sunglasses, I pushed the girls aside and just started hugging him and kissing him all over. I could hear him asking his fiancée: "Who is this? Who is this?!"

When I finally stopped hugging him and backed away, I took off my sunglasses and he finally realized it was his mom! All he could say was "WOW, WOW, and WOW!" And he kept repeating that one word all through the fifty-two mile drive back to our home! Richard, thank you for helping me to make his wedding day a dream come true . . . for both of us!

Love,
Mary Ann

Mary Ann's letter had me laughing out loud when I got to the part where her son didn't recognize her. It was such a whimsical story. I had to call her and say how much I enjoyed reading it! When I called the first time, she wasn't home . . . get this, she was out taking her "evening walk!"

This lady is just too good to be true, I thought to myself. I waited an hour, called again and this time sweet Mary Ann answered the phone.

"Richard," she said, "My son told me you called, well you *know* I couldn't believe it! I never had a famous person call me before!"

"Oh honey, I'm not famous, *you* are! Your pictures and your story . . . you are just adorable. How was your son's wedding?"

"Oh, it was beautiful, so beautiful," she said. "It had been raining off and on all week long but the day of the ceremony, the weather was just perfect. Everything was!"

Mary Ann told me that a friend of hers asked the groom what he thought of his mom's new look and he said, "Awesome, totally awesome!"

"And how far are you from your goal now?" I asked.

"Well, I want to lose about thirty more pounds but my goal is not so much on the scale. I set my goal with a dress size!"

I thought it was a very interesting approach and asked Mary Ann what that goal was.

"Oh, I started out a twenty-four and a half, I'm down now to a size fourteen and my final goal is a twelve."

"Wow, you're just a dress size away! What does your husband think of this big change?" I asked.

NEVER GIVE UP

"Your letter said he was kind of skeptical when you were starting out."

"Oh, I'm not the only person around this house with a new attitude." Mary Ann laughed a little when she told me that.

"What's so funny?" I asked.

"Well, before I lost the weight, he was sweet enough to me, he's a really good husband, you know. But after I lost all this weight, well . . . last week he bought a little present . . . a teddy!" Mary Ann and I howled! What a super lady. She really did add a bright spot to my day. She told me she knows she'll never look like Twiggy but you know what, I can't imagine Twiggy or anyone else being any happier than Mary Ann is these days, and what could be more important than that!

TRUTH OR CONSEQUENCES

If I should take a tiny taste
from someone else's plate
surely that would not affect
the balance of my weight.

And what about a little snack
while standing at the sink?
These calories don't matter,
is what I like to think.

As for all those little tastes
I like when it is dark
well if the food cannot be seen
how can it leave its mark?

Food that's nibbled from the fridge
deserves no second thought,
unless of course I'm careless
and I happen to get caught.

What about the food I eat
when I am home alone?
And what about a little snack
while talking on the phone?

These are times I like to think
that calories do not count
especially if I only eat
a very small amount.

How I wish it all were true
but I am sad to say
when any food goes past my lips
there is a price to pay.

Food has no free entry pass
however small the amount.
I may as well just face the truth
each calorie does count.

ANYTHING YOU CAN DO ...

Donna's Story

*M*y adult life has been devoted to helping those people that the majority of society "looks down on" or "feels sorry for." The truly apropos word though is *misunderstood*—I work with people who make others feel, for whatever reason, "uncomfortable." The group I'm best known for working with is the overweight. Because I relate to them so well, there is a strongly felt bond between me and the overweight. I've also reached out to our elderly population. I prefer calling them "silver citizens"—you know, our parents, our grandparents. It amazes me that the very group responsible for all of us being here has often been mistreated, neglected and sometimes even downright abandoned!

There is another group close to my heart—we call them handicapped or disabled. Here I like to say physically challenged or handicapable. A few years ago I wrote a book with them in mind called, *Reach for Fitness*. It contained exercises designed to help the physically challenged improve their physical well-being and also offered nutritional guidelines we should all follow. To produce this book, I gathered a team of experts from the top orthopedic hospital in Los Angeles. We sent out questionnaires to other hospitals, doctors and rehab centers across the country. We wanted a wide array of input from experts nationwide in creating the first comprehensive "textbook" of exercise and nutrition ever for this most important group of people. When you put together a project like this, always in the back of your head you hope that at least one person will benefit. Of course, you rarely get to meet or know any of those people. But I got lucky; I did get to meet one dynamic lady and this is her story!

Donna was only eighteen months old when the tests began to find out why she was having problems with the most basic movements such as standing, walking or raising her arms. The doctors didn't know what was causing her problems but after thorough testing diagnosed her condition as spinal muscular dystrophy.

This form of MD causes a slow but gradual deterioration of muscle tissue over time. As she got older, Donna's muscles would function less and less effectively. Her doctors could not determine how much or how fast that would happen. Donna's parents were advised to keep a close watch on her but at the same time, treat her like "an ordinary kid."

Her parents were determined she live as "regular" a life as possible, taking great care not to spoil or pamper her. Their efforts worked incredibly well. Even as a kid Donna was already demonstrating a certain "spark" that would light her path through life.

She was wearing leg braces by the time she entered a special school for children with other physical challenges, but could get around with the best of them. When she got home from her first day of school, she walked right up to her mother and asked, "Why did you send me to 'that' school? All the other kids there had something wrong with them, they weren't like me!" Her mom and dad knew the day would come when Donna would have to be "mainstreamed" with the rest of society and they started the process right at home. It was always paramount that their daughter learn, despite her limitations, to do her very best.

As she got older the muscular dystrophy was running its course, slowly diminishing Donna's mobility. An unfortunate accident on the way to church made her situation even more challenging. She fell and bent her foot so badly, that the damage was irreversible. Her braces had to be traded in for a wheelchair.

Now when I told you this girl had a "spark," I wasn't kidding! She went right on to public high school with all the other students who could walk, ride a bike and swing their hips at the school dance. And when graduation day came around, she was right up on that stage to pick up her diploma just like everybody else.

She didn't stop there. Donna enrolled at the University of Akron to continue her studies. That's where the problem with food started. Of course the transition from braces to wheelchair caused her to put on some weight. Reduced activity caused by not being able to use the lower part of her body would naturally cause a weight gain. But Donna was hitting the books hard, studying in the library, sitting all day in class—

RICHARD SIMMONS'

NEVER GIVE UP

she was moving much less and eating much more.

Her busier schedule made it difficult to eat regular and well-balanced meals like she used to. And after eating enough fast-food hamburgers, french fries and shakes, she actually started to prefer them to good food. Up until this point, she had never eaten this way! Donna graduated from college a lot smarter and a lot heavier. She got a job as a social worker but didn't do any work on her most important case: her body.

It wasn't that she didn't have any resource to confront this new "weighty" situation. Someone had given her a copy of my book, *Reach for Fitness* and she'd read it cover to cover. This is very impressive, she thought. They really put a lot of time and effort into this, what a great book! And that's all it was to her at the time—a great book. It sat collecting dust on her bookshelf for two years as she continued to satisfy her ever growing appetite.

Now Donna admits to this very day, "I'm very vain!" She had always taken great care to make sure her hair was perfect, along with the mascara, lipstick, the clothes she wore. I mean, this was a very together lady. But during and after the college days, she had witnessed her dress size graduate from size 12 up to size 22!

The increase in her girth was starting to get through to her brain, she knew she couldn't keep it up. Donna had some serious soul searching to do. After working so hard to jump over so many hurdles in life, why was she deliberately placing an extra hurdle in her way?

Donna never took herself or her situation in life so seriously that she couldn't joke about herself (a very good attitude, by the way!). She often refers to herself as having a "Supergimp mentality." That meant she

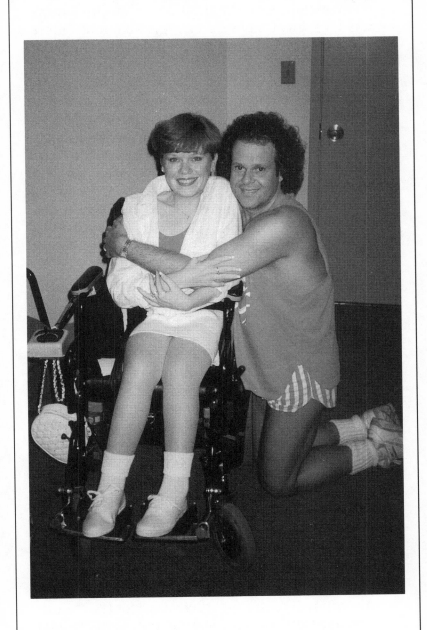

knew people would expect less of her due to their own perception of her limits as a person. But Donna always took great pleasure in being able to do more than what the world expected. Well, it was time again to do more!

Dusting off that old copy of my book, she read it all over again. The words for some reason seemed different this time, the pictures of people with braces, with one leg, in Wheelchairs, all exercising made more sense to her. "Why have I waited so long?" she wondered, "everything I need to get better has just been sitting here, waiting."

Donna began following the exercise and the nutritional advice in the book. She understood that even by exercising, the muscular dystrophy would prevent her muscles from getting any stronger but she could maintain the strength she had! Not only that, she could increase her body's range of motion; she was delighted with the results.

"No more hamburgers!" she declared. Donna completely kicked the junk food out of her life. From then on, whatever went into her body was going to have to give something back. Fried food was dead! Long live the broiler! She had broiled fish, broiled beef, more salads and smaller portions. (Do you ever eat while doing something else? Well, of course you do but have you ever thought about how many extra calories sneak into your stomach when you're not paying attention?) Donna began paying attention to what, why, where and when she ate and by doing so learned to appreciate her meals while eating less.

Her body was responding to this new way of life. She could get her heart rate up by lifting her arms, swinging her torso and working those neck muscles.

Now you will notice that there are a lot less "numbers" in this story. Because she couldn't stand, Donna didn't know her highest or present weight. What she did know was her dress size had come down from that size 22 to a size 8! Wow! And she looks downright petite.

Donna and I had been communicating through the mail and over the telephone. Our big meeting occurred on Cleveland's "Morning Exchange" talk show. Her story was too important not to be told and I told her she had to be there with me on the air. Her accomplishments were sure to light a fire to inspire people in and out of wheelchairs.

And she was eager to share her life when the host of the show introduced her to the audience. Donna grabbed that microphone, told us who she was and said, "I know you've heard this old saying many times . . . 'If I can do it, anybody can.' Well, it's true! My mobility and strength may be limited but I can exercise and I can lose weight. Please, don't ever use your limitations or any problem as an excuse . . . find out what your abilities are and use them to get whatever you need or want from life!" (Couldn't have said it better myself!)

Did you notice the word *depression* never came up in this story? I couldn't use it because it's not a word that applies when talking about Donna. She never felt there was anything wrong with her life in a wheelchair . . . that was just her! And she accepted herself.

There may be a "wheelchair" that's holding your life back. As you see, Donna never let it stop her. You can do one of two things . . . either sit around moping about how hopeless your situation is or you can challenge yourself and prove once and for all, "I can win my battle, I am capable!"

NEVER GIVE UP

THE BET
Cindy's Story

I was waiting in the car all the way in the back of the parking lot of the outlet mall where Cindy managed a store. She was going to be one of my latest "surprise visits" and I had done my homework. I knew she would be arriving to go on duty in about an hour which gave me plenty of time to go over all the letters and photos she'd sent me over the many months we'd been corresponding.

From the first letter she wrote me, I could see we had at least one connection. We both grew up with fathers who loved to cook! Cindy's father, Mick, learned from the best. Long before she was born he was in the merchant marines. While in the corps he was sent off to New York City's still elegant Waldorf-Astoria Hotel to learn culinary skills he'd use as a cook aboard the ship. Mick learned fast and while he was at sea for a few years had time to fine-tune his art. After his service was over, he returned to the mainland, started his family and never stopped what had become a true pleasure, cooking. The chef of the seven seas was now the chef in his own home. A meal at their home was more than that; it was a grand production.

Cindy was raised on things like mashed potatoes, but not made with milk; oh no, her father used real whip cream. His specialties included an assortment of beef dishes with thick, rich gravies. Some mornings he would get out of bed at 2:00, tiptoe to the kitchen and start baking bread, not just a loaf . . . several loaves. It took a lot to satisfy his troops.

The rest of the family might as well have turned off their alarm clocks on those days, they were awakened by the aroma of freshly baked homemade bread drifting through every room of the house. It's one of Cindy's fondest memories growing up. Everybody would make a mad dash to the kitchen to get in the "breadline." The loaves would be so warm that the butter, not margarine mind you, would melt away into each slice.

Nothing could have made Mick happier than to see his wife and kids not just well fed but fed on the best foods money could buy. Not only did he earn the bread, he also got to put it on the table. He was one of thirteen children growing up during hard times, his parents didn't have a lot of money. The meals he grew up on kept them alive and fairly healthy but not much more than that. He swore then that when he had a family of his own, they would never have to live that way. He truly kept his vow.

Mick made sure that never a morsel was wasted; at mealtime, as "president" of the "Clean Your Plate Club," his job was to make sure no one left the table until their plates were empty. To Cindy's father, food was love and she was loved a lot!

In sixth grade, she weighed 126 pounds and to make things worse, her last name was Holstein . . . like the cow! Of course, there were the constant "mooing" sounds the other kids at school would use to tease her.

As Cindy got older, she was tired enough of all the teasing to stop eating so much. Besides, she was starting to look at boys as something more than just little pests. In junior high school she had curbed her appetite enough to start growing up instead of out. At age fourteen, her great personality and trimmer new body were enough to catch the attention of Greg. They dated all the way through high school and were married shortly after graduation. Cindy became the mother of three handsome sons.

In her new home, Cindy carried on the family tradition at the dining room table, every meal was an event. Having inherited her father's cooking talents, she was a wizard in the kitchen. Safe and secure with a husband, children and nice home, the need to be concerned about her appearance diminished. Cindy was back to her old eating habits and the pounds she lost in school had come back to roost bringing memories of her father and his belief that food is love.

Well over 200 pounds, she didn't feel any really pressing need to lose any weight. Sure, people noticed and would make little remarks occasionally about "how she was letting herself go." But Cindy had a quick fix for her bruised feelings after one of those comments: she'd make a trip to her personal medicine cabinet—the kitchen.

Greg loved his wife now every bit as much as the day they were married but she looked a lot different

NEVER GIVE UP

than the woman to whom he'd said, "I do." It was like walking on eggshells for him knowing how sensitive she'd become but one day as he watched her snacking on leftovers from one of her luscious meals he couldn't keep quiet any longer. "Cindy, honey . . . you've really put on a lot of weight . . . I'm worried about you. Have you thought about maybe going on a diet . . . or something? I know it would make you feel better."

This was the first time Greg had ever said anything about her weight. Cindy went nuclear. How could he tell her anything so horrible, so insensitive. It wasn't like she weighed 500 pounds. She was absolutely outraged that her very own husband could stoop so low and talk to her that way! That was also the last time Greg ever said anything to Cindy about her weight! But having trained Greg to keep his thoughts about her size to himself, Cindy couldn't muzzle her other relatives so easily. At the annual family holiday get-together she was attacked from all sides. Some of the aunts, uncles and cousins at the get-together hadn't seen her in a while and let their opinions be known loud and clear.

"Cindy, I just cannot believe how fat you've gotten . . . you even walk different . . . you walk like a duck!"

"Cindy . . . my baby . . . let me look at you. You've got such a pretty face . . . if only you could lose some weight!"

Cindy held herself together the best she could throughout the evening's ordeal. Why do I even bother coming to these stupid things anyway, she thought. But the undeniable truth was that nothing anyone said to her was anything less than the truth. In her heart, she'd always wanted to lose weight and that night decided she'd show them all, her husband, the family and most importantly: herself! "I can lose this weight," she told herself, "I want to be the me outside that I feel inside!"

Cindy had already decided on how to accomplish her goal, just as though she knew this day was coming, that she would get the momentum somehow and "go for it." She had seen my commercials on TV many times over, they were nice to watch and she'd always imagined herself being one of those people on the screen with me. She had doubted herself too much to make that first move but not anymore. Cindy camped out in front of the TV until she found me on the air and she called right away to get her own Deal-A-Meal.

"Mom! Did you see this package that came for you today? It's been sitting here on the table ever since you got home," Christopher shouted to his mother.

Cindy ran to the living room from the kitchen where she'd been making dinner. She couldn't remember feeling so excited in a long time, maybe not since giving birth. And in a way, she was giving birth. I'm going to show the world a whole new me, she thought. As she opened the box in front of her son, he looked on curiously.

"What's that you're all excited over?" Christopher asked.

"It's my new Deal-A-Meal," she told him.

"Dial-A-What?"

"It's a weight loss program from Richard Simmons. I'm going to finally lose this weight," she explained.

Christopher had heard this one before, "You're gonna lose weight? Yeah, right! And I'm going to be president someday! I betcha a hundred bucks you don't do it!"

211   RICHARD SIMMONS'

Cindy couldn't believe what she was hearing! "Are you kidding, a hundred bucks? Okay, you're on! But I can tell you right now, you're gonna lose, buddy. Hey, but who knows . . . you may grow up to be president someday!"

Cindy was serious about what she wanted to do. She designed personal low calorie meals for herself while cooking a different meal for the family. She began exercising every day and had programmed the kids to know when it was time for her work out. At 8:00 every night, a "silent bell" went off and they vacated the rec room for an hour. That was her time to go in, pop in one of my exercise videos and boogie on down for the next sixty minutes!

Weeks of light eating and heavy exercise were producing the new downsized model of Cindy. It was 7:59 P.M., she was heading for the rec room, towel in hand, ready to sweat. On the way in she bumped into her youngest son, Keith. He stopped, gave her a longer look and said, "You know, Mom . . . you're really starting to look skinny!"

Cindy didn't know what to say, she was too happy to hear the compliment! So happy in fact, she cried all the way through her workout. None of her sons had ever seen their mother thin, but they would, she promised herself, they would!

As she kept losing weight, Cindy was losing something else, too: her wardrobe. Those size 24 dresses didn't fit anymore. To her they seemed to belong to someone else, so she would let someone else wear them. She couldn't afford to give them away so she tried another route, placing an ad in the local newspaper for a garage sale.

The rec room that had witnessed her transformation was converted into "Cindy's Department Store."

There was a dress department, activewear, out-erwear, and, of course, "better dresses." She even borrowed an old cash register from work and she was open for business. The "store" was open for only one day but Cindy made enough money to go out and buy herself a brand-new wardrobe!

I looked at my watch, sixty minutes of reminiscing had passed quickly and Cindy should have been walking into the store at any minute. I gazed at her "after" picture one more time to help me spot her. She looked so good after losing seventy-eight pounds! I looked out the window of the car and knew my wait was over as I watched that photo come to life. Cindy was arriving right on schedule. I pulled my cap down low over my head (my hair is always a dead giveaway!) and watched as she got out of her car, crossed the parking lot and walked into the children's clothing store she managed.

After a couple minutes, I also entered the store. The store was packed with shoppers. The customers didn't know what to think as I walked around the floor calling Cindy's name. Some of them said hello, others simply pointed. The store's real customers, the kids didn't know what to think!

Before things got too far out of hand, Cindy spotted me, "Richard," she screamed! "I don't believe this! Richard Simmons . . . what are you doing here?" She ran across the store and threw her arms around me! "You came to see me, I never thought in a million years this would happen to me. I'm so glad you're here!"

Leading me by the hand, she took me around the store and introduced me to each of her employees then we retreated to her office where we could share some private time. She told me how much better life

NEVER GIVE UP

was for her and thanked me for caring about people like her.

As I looked around the office, I saw pictures of the family everywhere. I picked up a photo of her and the boys, "Now which one of these guys bet you a hundred dollars you couldn't lose the weight?" I asked.

"Oh, that was Christopher," she laughed, pointing him out.

I asked if he ever paid up and she told me, "Oh yes, he certainly did! He works for me at the store and I docked his paycheck until the debt was paid in full!"

Now you and I both know, the hundred bucks she collected from Christopher was not important, that's not what Cindy really won. What she won was a new, healthier body, self-respect and confidence in what she could achieve with a made-up mind!

Say that again? Can't think of anybody you can place a bet with? Wrong! Bet YOURSELF that you can win whatever it takes to make you feel more complete. I'll bet you *can!*

THE PICNIC

Angela's Story

*H*ey look . . . it's Mama Cass!" That's what Angela heard every day on the playground at school. On the walk home, people in passing cars would sometimes slow down, and scream out, "Hey hippo!" This was a pretty tough way to spend the day for a teenager. How well I know! But when Angela finally got home, everything would be right in her world. She was always greeted by her mom, Fran, and a kitchen full of endless sugarcoated treats.

There were no food rules in this fine Italian home. Here, in its truest form, eating was always a joyous celebration. Diets were never mentioned and rude remarks about fat or weight were never heard.

At age sixteen, Angela made the brave decision to go on her first diet. All of her friends at school were on the then popular Stillman Diet, and they were all raving about it. The idea was great; you could eat as much protein as you wanted, followed by drinking lots of water. The result would be a quick loss of weight.

Angela lost seventy-five pounds on the diet. Everyone watched with amazement as she literally seemed to melt away. She was feeling great, had reached her goal and felt it was safe to "stop dieting." As you might guess, she went right back to her old eating habits and it wasn't long before she'd gained the weight back.

When Angela had to reach into the closet and take out all her old fat clothes again, she made herself a promise. She had seen her friends do the diet yo-yo for years. She certainly had no intention of becoming a member of *that* club.

She told herself, I won't ever try this again. I didn't learn anything from this and I made a fool of myself by gaining all my weight back. If my heart and mind are not together, I will never try to lose weight again!

Angela continued her life with that promise in mind. She ate whatever she wanted and as much as she wanted. At 242 pounds she married a wonderful man, Vincent. He had a son from a previous marriage and to Angela he was *her* son, too. She and Vincent also had a daughter together, a beautiful baby girl with the face of an angel, Sarah.

Angela followed in her mother's footsteps . . . right into the kitchen. She was an expert baker. Between Thanksgiving and New Year's Day, it was nothing for her to bake 138 dozen cookies . . . that's 1,656 cookies! Chocolate chip, lemon bars, sour cream, just name the cookie and Angela could turn it out of the oven for you.

Her favorite occasion for cooking was the annual

family picnic given by her cousin, Elaine. Everyone attending had to bring a main dish plus one dessert. Angela never missed the big event but it seemed there was a different Angela each year. There was the 250-pound Angela, the 350-pound Angela. Finally, the 425-pound version appeared.

The fatter Angela got, the stronger her appetite became. The last picnic she attended as the large version, Angela spent the whole day sampling as many dishes as she could. By the end of the day she was feeling pretty stuffed but not so stuffed that she wasn't the first person in line to grab the leftovers.

She bid farewell to everyone and drove home with a box full of chicken, hamburgers and an array of desserts from baklava to cheesecake to raspberry tarts. Angela put all her treats carefully away in the kitchen and went to bed.

After the alarm went off the next morning, she jumped out of bed and headed straight for the kitchen. Mmm, leftovers for breakfast, she thought, opening the fridge and taking out the goodies from yesterday's picnic. As she tried to decide what to have first, her concentration was broken by a phone call from her mother.

"What are you doing?" Fran asked, her usual morning question.

Angela replied, "Oh, I was just about to have a little breakfast."

"So what are you having?"

"Just some leftovers from yesterday," Angela told her mom.

Suddenly her mother was silent. She had bitten her tongue so many times in the past, but not this time.

"Angela, now you know I don't normally talk about your weight but my God, you are killing your-

self! You know our family has a history of heart problems, you know I have a history of heart problems, and yet you still eat like this. You have got to do something before it's too late!"

Angela's mother seemed almost to be begging—something she had never done before. Angela stared at her bounty of picnic leftovers but for some reason her hands couldn't reach for the food. Was Angela about to embark on another weight loss program? You bet she was! That phone call from Fran was the spark that finally jump started her heart and her mind together.

The leftovers remained in her kitchen untouched by Angela for several days until they had to be thrown out. She let them stay there because she wanted to prove to herself that she would not eat them. Even after all this time, thoughts of her failure with the Stillman Diet still haunted her. This time she was determined to do it right.

Angela finally came out from behind what she called her "food mask." She changed her eating habits and soon began to lose weight. First she simply ate only half of what she was used to. She continued to enjoy her favorite Italian dishes. Later she became conscious of how much fat was in her diet. The first hundred pounds came off quickly and Angela reached an exciting milestone. For the first time ever she could read her own weight on the scale at home. There was no more going to a friend's house for assistance or the doctor's office to get "the verdict of the scales."

Oh, Angela was still baking, too. Even she couldn't believe that 138 dozen cookies still got baked during the holidays but now she was able to resist the temptation of bingeing on her own creations.

NEVER GIVE UP

In her latest letter to me, Angela wrote that she was down to 198 pounds. She had not been under 200 pounds in twenty years and her total weight loss was now 227 pounds! I want to share the last paragraph of that letter with you:

> The new me not only makes *me* happy, it gives more life to my family. I did not realize that by being fat, I was not only killing me but also shortchanging my family. Richard, I must tell my son how sorry I am for depriving him of so much in life because of my fat. I just thank God that it's not too late for me and my daughter to share so many of life's experiences I did not pursue before.

ON THE ROAD AGAIN

Kathy and Frank's Story

A cruise was the last thing in the world Kathy needed right now! Trapped on a ship for over a week, with all that food, she'd never lose any weight!

Kathy's doctor had already put her on a strictly controlled diet of 400–800 calories a day and she'd lost forty-five pounds by sticking with it. But for reasons unknown to her or the doctor, the diet simply stopped working and she couldn't lose another ounce. Kathy was urgently seeking another way to get her "engine" running again and she wanted to do it before the cruise she and her husband, Frank, had planned!

Over the past ten years she'd gained ten pounds for each year of marriage. The multiplication was simple, she'd added 100 pounds and she wanted to turn those numbers around.

One of her neighbors had a copy of my Sweatin'
To The Oldies exercise videos and was loving it. She
suggested Kathy give it a try, maybe exercise was the
missing link to her success. Taking the advice, Kathy
got a copy of the video and sure enough, by working
out with it daily the pounds started to come off again.

The cruise date was rapidly approaching. She and
Frank were to drive from their home in Sacramento
down to the port at Los Angeles to board the ship
bound for Mexico. Kathy did not intend to allow
herself to fall off the program while she was away
from home.

She had heard about my exercise studio in L.A.
and told Frank she'd like to stop by since they would
be in the area anyway. Having done so well with
my Sweatin' video, she thought there might be more
motivational aides available at my studio.

When they arrived at the club, Kathy was a little
disappointed that I wasn't there in person. "It would
have been kind of nice to see Richard," she told the
assistant manager, Judy.

"Well if you're in town tonight and you're not
busy, why don't you come by again?" Judy told her.
"Richard will be here teaching class tonight."

Frank, knowing how much it meant for his wife to
see me volunteered, "Tell you what, we'll spend the
day at Disneyland and swing back by here in time for
you to see Richard. How's that?"

Kathy was thrilled! After a full day at The Magic
Kingdom, they returned to Slimmons for our first
meeting.

That night in class, between exercises, I kept noticing this lady's face bobbing in and out of the "port-
hole" windows in the door separating the workout
room from the club's lobby area. I know all the mem-

bers at my club but this was a new face and I wondered why she was *out there* instead of *in here* sweating with the rest of us.

Class ended and I walked out into the lobby and talked with some of the members as I always do following a workout. My mystery lady was still there and she seemed nervous. After most of the other members had filed out, Judy saw I was free and brought Kathy and Frank over to introduce us.

Kathy shared her story with me as Frank stood on the sidelines; you could tell he was not much of a talker. But Kathy made up for him! She told me she was losing weight with my program but her biggest problem was staying motivated. "What can I do to keep myself on track?" she asked.

Pointing to our exercise room, I told her, "Well, you can start by walking through *that* door and joining us the next time you're here!"

Kathy explained that they lived in Sacramento, over 400 miles away and coming to my class on a regular basis would be just short of impossible. Of course I understood the distance was a major problem and advised her to keep using the exercise tapes. "You can do this," I insisted and made her promise to write and keep me posted on her progress.

The next morning Kathy and Frank departed on their ship to Mexico. Being careful not to indulge, she watched what she ate, took advantage of any exercises the ship had to offer and actually *lost* one pound! Now if you're thinking, "one pound, big deal," then you obviously have never taken a cruise. Those boats are like floating buffets!

Kathy was proud that she'd done so well on the trip but back home in Sacramento, she couldn't stop thinking about her visit to Slimmons. She wanted to

NEVER GIVE UP

come back and take one of the classes. She wondered if Frank would drive her back down.

Well Frank thought she was out of her mind! "Look, Kathy," he told her, "I understand how much you wanted to do this but it's over four hundred miles down to Los Angeles . . . and you want to go back *just* to take an exercise class? Come on now, be reasonable!"

Disappointed by her husband's reaction, Kathy made up her mind that when Frank got home that night she was going to tell him she was going to Los Angeles with or without him.

When Frank got home, Kathy prepared to drop her bombshell but before she could even bring it up, Frank had some news of his own.

"Kathy, I did some thinking while I was at the office today," he said. "You've worked so hard to lose this weight and you've done so well . . . if anybody deserves this trip, it's you. When do you want to go?"

Kathy gave her husband a big bear hug and could hardly contain her excitement! The very next Friday they filled the tank, hopped on Interstate 5 and headed south for Los Angeles. Arriving just after dark, they checked into a hotel near my studio and Saturday morning, there they were, not just bystanders this time. The *both* of them worked out to song after song with the rest of the class. Frank discovered he liked exercise, too, and thus a new weekend ritual was born!

Every Friday afternoon now they follow the same routine on route to L.A. Listening to my motivational tapes on the way, they drive straight through the San Joaquin Valley to the little town of Buttonwillow. That's where they stop to fill up, take a short break and have a "lite dinner" at the local Carl's Jr. restaurant. Kathy has the "skinny baked potato" without all the extras along with a little chicken salad. Frank likes the salad bar. After dinner it's a fairly short drive the rest of the way into L.A.

Kathy has lost 105 pounds and Frank is a complete convert, he's lost 56 pounds! Those weekend trips have not only helped their waistlines but their marriage as well. Closed up in a car for seven hours of continuous driving, well, you have lots of time to work out any family debates!

I look forward to seeing them on Saturday mornings. Frank, who was so withdrawn when I first met him, has come out of his shell. Kathy brags about how much she likes herself now. "When I look into the mirror these days, the lady looking back at me is smiling!"

Interstate 5 slices a straight line through the central California desert with very little scenery along the way. A lot of people call the route boring. But to Kathy and Frank, well it's like their own personal "freeway of love!"

NEVER GIVE UP

I am a **terrific person** and I like myself **right now**, no matter what I weigh.

◆

The next time I have a **craving** for anything I know is fattening or am tempted not to exercise, I will think about the **new me**, and I will be strong.

◆

I will take a look **in the mirror** and say, "I'm going to have a **great day**."

◆

SEE/SAW/SEE NANCY NOW!

Nancy's Story

*N*ancy's first marriage broke up because of food. "Who do I love the most, my husband or my food?" That was the question Nancy had to ask herself. The answer: "my food!" She admits, "My own self-loathing affected those around me and I let my high school love go in lieu of food!"

Only twenty-four years old at the time, and now weighing in at 200 pounds, Nancy did not want to remove herself from the social scene. But if she was going to have any luck at all in getting a date, she was going to have to lose some weight first. Ironically with her marriage over, she finally had to give up her "first love." Using a starvation diet, her weight declined from 200 down to 110 pounds.

After meeting and marrying her new husband, Paul, Nancy was soon expecting her first baby. Knowing that almost all women gain weight in pregnancy, Nancy didn't worry about letting herself go. She saw pregnancy as "carte blanche" to eating heaven! She slipped back into her old eating habits and regained every pound she'd lost and then some.

Of course, Nancy was very depressed about backsliding and the only solace she found from the bad moods was in the new baby's smile *and* more food.

Nancy returned to her career with Blue Cross after the baby was born. Following a big promotion to marketing representative, she was yanked from the back of the office and placed directly in the public eye. The job meant a lot to her. But only five feet tall and weighing 228 pounds, she needed to lose weight again, not to improve her social life this time, but instead to project a proper professional image for the company.

Using the same starvation technique that had worked for her after the divorce, she lost eighty-four pounds in four months, almost the exact amount she'd lost the first time around. As is usually the case with these crash diets, the weight loss didn't last, Nancy's numbers were on the way up again within a year. By the time her second baby was born, those lost eighty-four pounds had found their way home!

Now a two-child family, Paul and Nancy decided it would be better if she left her job and stayed home to take care of their two daughters. The transition from working mom to housewife was not an easy one to make. To keep busier around the house as well as bring in extra income, Nancy started an in-home child care business.

Gone were the days that she got up in the morning, styled her hair, applied makeup and selected the perfect outfit for a busy day at the office. A house full of kids didn't care how she looked and Nancy reached the point where she didn't care either.

Her new beauty regimen consisted of grabbing the first comfortable thing she could find in the closet, splashing a little water on her face and preparing to meet the children.

Each morning after all the other moms dropped off their little ones, Nancy made sure they had breakfast, played with their toys and got their afternoon naps. The TV was on most of the day and when the children weren't watching, she would watch whatever was on.

There were many days she would see my shows and watch as I interviewed people who had lost weight. She did love what I had to say and what I was doing for others, but out of frustration, she would always end up switching the channel. Those programs forced her to consider her own appearance and she was not at all ready to face her own weight problem.

The child care business was going great but Nancy missed her old job. She resented the fact that she was making it possible for those other moms to leave the house and go off to work. That's where *she* belonged and would have been more than willing to trade places with any one of them.

Nancy truly loved children but didn't feel as useful and productive as she once did. While the kids were taking their naps one afternoon in early spring, Nancy found herself particularly depressed and turned to the favorite room in the house to soothe herself: the kitchen. She continued putting herself down as she binged on one snack after another.

The food didn't drive away the depression this time. Nancy kept thinking and her depression grew

NEVER GIVE UP

deeper as she analyzed point by point all the negatives in her life. She left the kitchen and went to the bedroom. There was a full-length mirror she'd avoided for years and she took a good honest look at the now 248-pound woman staring back at her.

"I saw a freak looking back at me! All the feelings of anguish surfaced. The feeling of never fitting in or being treated like a substandard human being . . . praying I would never get sick so I wouldn't have to go to a doctor's office and get on a scale. I remembered all the good times I'd missed because I had nothing to wear and being too embarrassed to be seen. I missed taking part in school activities with my daughters, ashamed that I wasn't small and pretty like all the other moms!"

But what Nancy remembered most of all were all the thousands of times she had cried out to God or anyone who could to . . . "please help me!" At that moment, Nancy felt she had nothing else to live for. Her very sanity had been replaced by one single desire for relief; Nancy wanted to feel relief!

The children were all still safely asleep when Nancy walked to the garage. Tears streamed down her face as she closed and locked the door from the inside. She started a frantic search for some old rags to stuff into the tailpipe of the car.

With the tailpipe securely plugged, she got into the car, rolled up the windows and held the ignition keys in her hand. She wanted to start the car up but before she could, her mind had another montage of images to play out for her.

"Through my tears I saw my husband's face on the day we said our wedding vows. I remembered our awe as we held our baby daughters in our arms for the first time. I remembered brushing my twelve-year-old's long, silky blond hair the night before. And I could hear my little three-year-old say as she hugged me before leaving to visit a friend that morning . . . 'I love you, Mommy, I'll see you later.' "

Shaking, frantic and embarrassed, Nancy ran back into the house in hysterics but thanking God for her life, realizing she had plenty of things to live for! She also remembered how much better she felt about herself when she wasn't obese. Nancy was unhappy with the way she looked but knew how good she *could* look! Having lost weight before, the wrong way, this time Nancy was determined to get it right!

She thought back to my TV show, people losing weight with Deal-A-Meal and my exercise videos. She had enough dieting experience to adapt the Deal-A-Meal and exercise videos even though she didn't yet have them. Nancy decided to consider me her cheerleader and coach.

Years of diet experience had made her somewhat of a pro at the game. She had always known the *right* way to lose weight, with a healthy, well-balanced food program. But her problem in the past was she'd always opt for the quick fix and try to lose all the weight overnight.

Getting on a solid food exchange program, Nancy attended group meetings for a while but couldn't work them into her hectic daily schedule. Having to give up the meetings didn't stop her from continuing the program at home, though.

With eyes on the goal and on the TV, she tried never to miss any of my appearances. The advice and encouragement she saw me give to others became advice for Nancy! Even though we didn't know each

NEVER GIVE UP

other, she felt I was proud of the great job she was doing losing weight. (By the way, she could see into the future—I *am* proud of her!)

Resisting the ever present temptation to cheat, Nancy's girlish figure was returning. Seeing the results of her labor we added incentive to keep going.

"As I surpassed each hurdle," she told me, "the next hurdle was that much easier and I found myself dealing with birthdays and holidays with a new discipline and confidence rather than what I call 'scale-aphobia' for the morning after!"

And now, let me present the new Nancy . . . with her biggest single weight loss ever, 112 pounds!

"I am living again," she wrote me. "I chaperon dances at my thirteen-year-old's school. I teach part-time at my four-year-old's preschool. I go out, I smell the grass early in the morning and walk in the rain. I see the birds, the flowers and children's smiles. I am so grateful to be alive with the new quality of life I've given myself."

The reasons for Nancy's diets are important to examine: the first time she lost weight to get a husband; the second time to impress her boss. The third diet was charmed because she did it for herself. And even though she lost weight the "wrong" way the first two times around—by starving herself—the important thing to remember is that she tried.

So many of us fail once and give up thinking, I can't do it, I'm a flop! But so what if you stumble? Do what Nancy did: pick yourself up, brush yourself off and try, try again. *Never give up!* Nancy felt *she* was worth it and as I tell you all the time—so are *you!*

ONE PILL MAKES YOU SMALLER

Terry's Story

*T*erry had been diligently saving his lunch money from school and any other money he could earn for over a month. He wasn't saving to buy a present for his mom or a cool new jacket for himself. Terry was saving his money to buy diet pills.

The senior class trip was coming up, he was already one of the biggest kids in high school at 204 pounds. He'd promised himself to lose forty of them in time for the trip.

A friend from school had another friend who could get the pills for him. Twenty dollars would get you a month's supply and Terry was ready to make his purchase. He made plans to meet his contact after school near the football field. Terry felt like he was in a James Bond movie during their secret transaction as he exchanged money for a miracle.

The deal was made and Terry held the tiny white pills in his hand. Losing forty pounds for the senior trip should be no problem now. Just one pill a day and it was no problem at all. With his appetite artificially suppressed, in less than two months he dropped down to 165 pounds! He was in fine shape when the bus pulled away from Lake City High loaded with him and his classmates. Terry even managed to keep the weight off for a while.

After graduating from high school he enrolled in classes at Tennessee Technological University. He quit school after getting a job working for a local electronics company. Terry got on-the-job training and there were excellent benefits and excellent pay so Terry decided it wasn't worth going to college now that he was making great money right here with only a high school diploma.

Those were good days for Terry: good job, good pay and he was still managing to watch his weight fairly well. The bad news was the party wouldn't last long. He was laid off from his great job after only six months. The company closed its doors abruptly and moved operations to another state.

After having things go so well and then evaporate so suddenly, Terry got so depressed that he turned to his old standby to make himself feel better: he got very careless and started eating again. In just five months he gained back his lost forty pounds plus a few extra ones. He hated himself for regaining the weight and since he was still out of work, there was no motivation for him to lose it. He spent his time looking for a new job and when he wasn't looking for work, he was eating as much food as he wanted.

When he finally did find employment it was at a local grocery store and only paid the minimum wage. But with his unemployment checks ending, minimum wage was better than nothing. For a whole year, he stocked shelves, bagged groceries and rang up sales and pounds. All the while working at the store, he circulated applications at local businesses hoping something better would come his way.

That better job finally came through. Terry got a new job at another electronics plant; the pay wasn't as good as his first job but it was certainly a whole lot better than minimum wage. It seemed like those gray skies were finally clearing up. After one year on a dead-end job, he was feeling better about himself except for one thing, his weight had already zoomed up to nearly 300 pounds! He was ready to tackle the problem. His thought was that now that his job search was behind him, it was a good time to get back in shape.

But this time there was no school yard buddy to rescue him with a magic pill. But that wasn't going to stop Terry who decided to find a diet doctor. He was determined to lose weight! And the pills had worked before. He made a few calls around town until he found the man he was looking for.

"Yes sir, you certainly do have a weight problem, all right," the doctor commented as Terry sat in the examination room. "Do you have any idea how bad this is for your heart? You've really got to learn to take better care of yourself. You know, God only gives us one body, now drop your pants and bend over." Terry winced as the doctor pushed a needle into his backside. "Now that little shot will start you on your way. When you leave here, I want you to stop by a pharmacy and get this prescription filled."

On the way home, Terry's first stop was at the nearest drugstore he could find. He sat in the car and looked at his "medicine." Humph . . . they're green diet pills this time, he thought. Oh well, I don't care

NEVER GIVE UP

about the color as long as they get the job done!

The second batch of pills worked just as well as his first. In just two months he dropped fifty pounds and felt great. He had a good job again, was losing weight and even decided to enroll in classes at a nearby community college.

It was like the old days just after high school. Things can't get any better than this, he thought . . . but they could get worse! After a weekend trip with his best friend, Mary Ann, Terry got home and went to work on Monday morning to discover that he had been laid off.

"Great . . . another pink slip! I really don't need this!" He couldn't believe his misfortune. Two good jobs lost in less than four years, what next? Well, there were more unemployment checks and more reasons to return to the one thing in his life that was a constant . . . the one thing in his life that he could always depend on, no matter what . . . Terry "employed" his appetite again, full-time!

The problem was that the more he came to depend on food, the more he would neglect himself. It was a vicious cycle: he ate; he felt bad about himself then "punished" himself with neglect; then he would eat to "feel better." What a roller coaster! He dropped out of his classes at school and put all his effort into getting back into the work force. His good luck at finding jobs was almost even with his bad luck losing them. When he got a call from a nearby Boeing plant, his attitude swung back into the positive column. He got his best paying job yet assembling parts for airplanes. As he'd done in the past when good fortune struck, Terry felt that nagging urge to get his body back "on line." Another year had passed between jobs and he was at his highest weight ever, 363 pounds! Time to see the doctor!

This time the pills were red and it was exactly the color Terry was seeing. He felt like his body was not under his control. "Why do I keep losing weight this way?" he wondered. "I feel like some kind of drug addict. Pop a pill, lose a pound, gain it back, pop another pill . . . there's got to be a better way!" He knew that without real help, he'd either keep on gaining weight, end up in the hospital or die! But Terry took that next month's supply of pills home anyway; a better way would just have to wait.

Terry comes from a big family, I mean "big" in number. He had ten brothers and sisters! They were all very close and got along splendidly. He knew they were always concerned about his weight but usually would keep quiet about his constantly changing body sizes. And Terry could never tell them about his dependency on diet pills. He was too ashamed.

Terry was more than anxious for help but was so used to taking pills. It was the only way he knew. He had trapped himself in a dangerous cycle.

When his good friend Mary Ann called up and invited him out to dinner, Terry was delighted to hear from her. They had been best friends since high school, even commuted to classes together at Tennessee Tech. Mary Ann also enjoyed doing "fork lifts" every bit as much as he did. They had enjoyed many a fine meal together at her family's restaurant, Weaver's Country Kitchen, over in Lake City. They specialized in the best down-home cooking around, food like country biscuits with gravy, southern fried chicken, catfish and hush puppies. There was always good eating at Weaver's!

But Mary Ann had a surprise in store for Terry that evening when she picked him up. "Mary Ann . . ." he asked, "You've lost weight, haven't you?"

237   RICHARD SIMMONS'

NEVER GIVE UP

"Well, thanks for noticing, Terry. I've lost twenty-one pounds, in fact!"

Terry was impressed. "Twenty-one pounds! How did you do it? Did you take pills or something?"

"Pills . . . oh no, not me! I'd be too scared! Have you seen Richard Simmons' Deal-A-Meal on TV?"

"Oh sure," Terry replied. "Is that how you did it?"

"Uh-huh, a friend from work swears by it, and she looks great so I decided to try it for myself. You can see the results! Here," she said, reaching into her purse. "Let me show you how it works." After a brief demonstration, they left for dinner. Terry watched as Mary Ann ordered a soup and salad, he was embarrassed he'd chosen a hamburger, fries and strawberry pie for dessert. Mary Ann kept quiet, she knew how sensitive she had been about her own weight and didn't want to hurt Terry's feelings.

After dinner he confided in Mary Ann. "I have to admit how depressed I was with you in there, maybe this program can work for me. God knows I'm ready to do it. I just can't 'live' in this body anymore, if you can call this living!" Terry got his own Deal-A-Meal program and prepared to make a "new deal" with himself!

He also got a set of my motivational tapes and was in his car when he listened to them for the first time. He couldn't believe his ears: "You know you are a compulsive eater if you always eat off someone else's plate. . . . Do you eat while shopping in the supermarket? . . . Do you think eating in a dark theater, those calories don't count? . . . Do you keep food in the car?"

Terry almost drove off the road when he heard that last one, there was an open bag of Ruffles lying on the backseat! I can't believe this, that's me he's describing, he thought. It's taken me this long to see myself! Terry may have been driving and watching the road through tears but he was determined more than ever to retake his body and his mind from the dark world of diet pills he'd locked himself in!

Now Terry is a great cook and I can personally tell you that all southerners love our style of cooking! But Terry found ways to compromise, he gave up his fried chicken for baked chicken, instead of making his green beans with fatback, he steamed them with herbs and spices. And from now on when he baked his famous three-layer coconut cake, he'd have one thin slice and let one of his brothers or sisters have the rest.

You know, if you're gonna lose, you're gonna have to exercise! Terry sweated six days a week with one of my tapes and loved every minute of it.

He was losing weight without a pill or a shot and this time, each pound he lost meant something because this time he had earned it! He kept a chart of his progress to help keep him going and as a reminder of how far he'd come.

After he'd lost his first seventy-five pounds, Terry went shopping for new clothes at the mall over in Oak Ridge. He noticed one of those big scales at the mall, you know, the ones that tell you to "have a nice day" along with your weight and though he knew how much he'd lost already, it's always nice to be reminded.

Getting aboard the scale, he popped in his quarter and was about to get the results when a group of kids walked by. One of them laughed and said to him, "It'll probably say 'one at a time, please!' " Terry still weighed 290 pounds, but he had lost seventy-five! He wished he could yell out at the kid who taunted him, "Hey, you don't know where I've come from!" But it was too late, the group of boys had disappeared into the mall.

Terry was a little down as he got off the scale. It felt almost like a setback but he turned his blues right back around and asked himself, what am I getting upset for? So I've got more work to do. But they ain't seen nothing yet! With that, Terry continued the march toward his goal, an insult from some stranger was not going to force him to give up!

Terry wrote me the most wonderful letter after he'd lost 132 pounds. "This is the first time in my life that I've lost weight without shots, liquid diets or pills. The wonderful thing about this time is that I did it with sound nutrition, exercise and keeping myself motivated! I haven't reached my goal yet but I have every confidence that I will and with flying colors!"

It was time for me to make a phone call! Terry's letter and pictures were fabulous. I've seen so many success stories over the years but each one is so unique to me. I needed to tell Terry personally, "Good job!"

When I reached him, Terry said, "Yep, I'm still on the program and doing really good! I'm gaining more self-esteem with every pound lost!"

"Well you keep right on losing," I told him. "I'll be checking in with you to see how you're doing!" A few months later I did call back. It was a Sunday afternoon and Terry had a house full of company. He told me their Baptist church was only a half mile away and a lot of his family members often got together at his house for an after service social.

"But don't worry," he told me, "I'm not touching any of the fried chicken. I have my own healthy local stash of food in the kitchen!"

Terry had kept the promise to himself to stay on

the program, he'd lost a total of 160 pounds and was down to 203. It was his lowest weight since the first day of his senior class!

"I'm in the driver's seat now," he said. "I can go

RICHARD SIMMONS'
NEVER GIVE UP

left, go right, put on the brakes or stay on the road! And because I'm in control . . . I choose to stay on the road from now on!" I asked him how his good friend, Mary Ann, was doing on the program and he was happy to report the news.

"Oh, she's still doing real good," he said, "as good as me. We're running neck and neck on total pounds lost!"

"You're kidding," I said. "Can I have her phone number? I'd love to call her, too!" Terry gave me Mary Ann's number and I dialed as soon as I hung up from talking with him.

"Hello."

"Mary Ann?"

"Yes?"

"Hi, Mary Ann, this is Richard Simmons. I just got off the phone with Terry, he told me you've both lost a whole lotta weight!"

"Oh Richard, aren't you so nice to call me," she replied. "Well, Terry's right, I had a twenty-pound head start but he has caught up with me. We've both lost right at one hundred sixty pounds!"

I thanked her for introducing Terry to the program and told her what a special team they were for motivating each other. She told me how she's the star at the office these days. Every day she gets more compliments on how much better her looks and attitude are.

She and Terry were planning a weekend trip to Atlanta to see their favorite singer, Elton John. They can't wait to see each other so they can compare their two new figures. It's been awhile since they were together. Mary Ann lives four hours away in another state. Now let's see, I wonder what their favorite Elton John song will be. Oh! I know! It's gotta be "Tiny Dancer"!

SHAPE, RATTLE AND ROLL!

Resa's Story

*M*y secretary, Marilyn, and I were sitting in the office answering mail when we heard the familiar beeeeep, signaling there was a fax transmission coming through. We finished the letter I was dictating and she walked over to retrieve the fax.

"What came over?" I asked.

"It's from *Shape* magazine," she replied. "It's about a lady who wrote an article on how she lost weight. Looks like you were mentioned in her article."

Marilyn handed me the fax from my friend, Cathy, the special projects editor at *Shape*. The story she faxed me was about Resa.

Each month, *Shape* spotlights a different person who has an inspirational weight loss story to share. In addition to publishing that person's success story, they also fly them to some exotic location for a "fitness holiday." Resa had got a fabulous holiday in Cancun.

Resa had mentioned me in her success story. She said that I had been her inspiration and felt that I cared about her struggle. Because I'd meant so much to Resa during her fight, Cathy wanted to know if I would be kind enough to make Resa's day by calling or writing to congratulate her on a job well done. Well, of course I'd call her! I called Cathy at *Shape*'s headquarters here in Los Angeles.

"Hi Cathy, it's Richard Simmons, I just got your fax and would just love to give Resa a call if you'll give me her phone number!"

"Oh Richard, you are a regular doll," Cathy said to me. "I know that Resa will be absolutely thrilled!" She started giving me the phone number, "Let's see . . . oh, here it is . . . area code 508 . . ."

I stopped her. "Five-oh-eight . . . where is that?" I asked. I've called so many of you over the years, heck, I thought that I knew every area code in the country by now! But this was a new one.

"Five-oh-eight is outside Boston," Cathy told me.

The little light bulb clicked "on" over my head again; that darn thing is always going off! It went off this time because I knew I would be in the Boston area in just a few weeks appearing at the Emerald Square Mall out in the suburbs. I figured Resa's house or place of employment would have to be close enough for me to go a giant step closer than a simple phone call. I wanted to work out a way to give her a big hug and much deserved "gold star" in person!

I told Cathy I would need her help to do it; of course, she was happy to oblige. I wanted to know where Resa worked, what time she got in, when she went to lunch, hey . . . there're a lot of bases to cover when you go "undercover." I also asked Cathy if she would send me a copy of Resa's personal story. It always helps to know as much as possible about my "surprises!"

When I got Resa's story and pictures in the mail I almost said *Wow*, right out loud! She was a pretty lady before she lost weight and she was even prettier now. But it was her story that really impressed me!

Back during her high school days, Resa had one of those petite little figures that everyone envies. She admitted that back then, "I was just too busy to over-eat. I grew up in a physically active family. We all loved to dance, run, walk and bicycle. There was no time in my life for excess food." After she was married though, Resa made up for lost time and found plenty of time to eat; she and her new husband simply could not get along.

Resa had always enjoyed taking a pen in her hand to write poetry, essays or short stories. But she never had enough nerve to submit them to any publications and now her husband would always ridicule what she had written. Instead of encouraging her to submit her work, he would say how childish or silly her writings were. That hurt, her words were important; her words were a part of Resa and her husband's constant put-downs of her talent were also a put-down of Resa. She turned to food as an outlet for her crushed feelings.

She says, "I ate and ate while my husband worked and worked, that way we didn't have to deal with our problems or each other!"

By the time her first child, Alan, was born, Resa had gained sixty pounds. Naturally that bothered her but all her relatives told her, "Oh, don't worry . . .

NEVER GIVE UP

you just gained some weight with the baby, you'll lose it as soon as the baby is born." Her relatives were wrong, Resa gained more weight.

When she was five months' pregnant with her second baby, she couldn't take the mental abuse anymore and separated from her husband. She went through her second pregnancy without her husband and with her little son to deal with. To help cope with the depression, she ate her way through that pregnancy until her second son, Jerome, was born. By then Resa was up to 225 pounds but she hadn't peaked yet, her bad eating habits continued and she gained fifty more pounds in two years. After Jerome's birth, she and her husband decided to give their marriage another try.

Resa was still overeating and very obese. She had gained so much weight, she stayed away from her five-year high school reunion. How could she show her body now? Everyone would be expecting that size 5 body she kept during her high school days.

"I knew everyone would talk about it and I didn't want to be the topic of that kind of conversation!" Resa was avoiding a lot of other things in her life; it was just easier to stay home, try to be a good mother to her boys and a good wife. When her oldest son became ill and had to have two surgeries, Resa had to spend even more time at home to care for him. Not that she minded, her kids were the most important people in her life.

Alan's second surgery was serious enough that afterward Resa had to carry him up and down the stairs of their home to the bathroom. One day while carrying him upstairs, she suddenly couldn't catch her breath! "My chest tightened and I nearly dropped him! I was convinced that I was having a heart attack!"

That incident left Resa very frightened, she decided it was time to lose weight before she died of a heart attack for real in the future. "I didn't want to miss being there to watch my children grow up!"

Resa had a most unique way of starting her weight loss program. On the first two days, she ate as much as she did on one of her "regular" days. But she did something different, she kept a log of everything she ate and at the end of the day got a calorie counter and a calculator and tallied up her day's total. She was eating way over 4,500 calories a day! (Let me point out here, that's twice as many calories an average size woman needs to maintain a healthy weight!) From that point on she began to cut back and count every calorie that slipped past her lips. But she didn't starve herself, so she wouldn't feel like she was being punished for trying to make her life better, she devised a little "reward" system.

Resa would buy one of her favorite treats, Chee•tos, in one of those big industrial sized bags. You know the ones! Then she would separate that big bag into several little one-ounce servings and put them in plastic Glad bags. She would have just one of them every now and then for being so good and staying on the program! (Very clever idea, Resa!)

After she lost the first twenty pounds, she could barely see the difference but knew the pounds were coming off and felt like "she was on a roll." She added exercise to her plan and still remembers huffing and puffing during her sit-ups with little Alan and Jerome sitting on her ankles!

As Resa continued shedding pounds, the rumblings she heard were not in her stomach: they were in her marriage. Her husband didn't care much at all for the new person she was becoming physically and he liked her new mental attitude even less.

When she had gained weight, her self-esteem was the only part of her that didn't grow. But as she got smaller, she started to like herself all over again. That meant she was finding it tougher to put up with her husband's demanding attitude toward her. She started to speak up where she used to simply shut up! Resa didn't want to cause a fight, she was just looking to have an identity, to be her own person. Her efforts to stand up for herself, even in the "kindest and gentlest" of ways did not work. She and her husband ended up calling it quits for good this time: they were divorced.

By that time, though, the new Resa had come out of the cocoon: she had lost 150 pounds! "It was amazing—a whole person was gone!" she wrote, "I changed my eating habits, I only ate when I was hungry. I was riding a bike again, racewalking, hiking, playing with my boys and even swimming. I had learned that life was to be savored; it wasn't meant to be a torment!"

I couldn't wait to meet her!

Cathy, my friend back at *Shape*, had done a very thorough job of getting me all the dish I would need to surprise Resa! She worked for an insurance agency outside Boston and I had cleared part of a busy day running from TV show to radio show to sneak up on her.

I got almost to the front door of her office building and stopped (that little light bulb again). I really should stop and pick up some pretty flowers for Resa!

I tell you it took some doing! I was running out of time and couldn't find a flower shop anywhere after having passed ten dozen hamburger places and another 200 video stores. I was really close to the line, time-wise, afraid I'd miss her schedule or my next appearance and out of desperation, I stopped at a service station for help. The attendant was surprised to see me.

"Hey, you're Richard Simmons! What in the world are you doing way out here?" he asked. "Are you lost or something?"

I told him he was close and explained why I was in the area and that I wanted to find a florist so I could take flowers to my friend. But I was also short of time and was about ready to give up!

"Flower shop," he replied, "why there's one three blocks down, right hand side of the street!"

"Yahooo!" I shouted. I thanked the kind attendant and zipped down the street, picked up a dozen pink roses then dashed back to Resa's office!

I walked through the doors and over to the receptionist. I had my finger over my mouth going, "Shhhh." In the quietest voice I could muster (and you know that's a strain for me) I explained why I was there and asked if she could point me in the right direction to get to Resa.

She replied in a whisper, "Back there . . . fourth cubicle by the window!" I grabbed and kissed her hand and walked quietly and quickly toward my target. In the fourth cubicle sat a cute, shapely blond just talking away on the telephone, her back was facing me.

"Excuse me . . . excuse me . . ." I said in a deep voice. "Uh, delivery for . . ."

Resa raised her hand as if to signal to whoever was behind her to be quiet!

"Uh, excuse me . . ." I tried again. "Excuse me, delivery . . ."

It was Resa's turn to say, "excuse me" to the person on the other end, she put her hand over the mouthpiece, swung around in her chair and to this day I think she was about to let me have it! As she swung around, her face had a rather stern expression that changed to shock as she saw me standing there holding the flowers and looking as innocent as I possibly could!

I dropped to my knees presenting her the flowers and said, "I'm so sorry for interrupting you, I just wanted to give you these."

Resa took her hand from the mouthpiece of the phone, "Uh, you know what . . . can I get back to you . . . I believe this is Richard Simmons standing . . . no . . . actually kneeling here in front of my desk . . . uh-huh . . . yeah . . . that Richard Simmons! Yeah . . . I promise . . . I promise, I'll try and explain later!" Resa hung up the phone.

"These flowers are for you," I told her. "I'm so glad you felt like I was part of your success!" Resa and I had a wonderful time together. I explained to her how I'd come to visit her and she thanked me for taking the time.

"Richard, whenever I saw you on TV, you were such an inspiration. It was like having you with me every step of the way!"

We hugged, we cried, we swapped stories, we said good-bye, but we still stay in touch. Resa wrote me a few weeks ago, she's still getting feedback from *Shape*'s article about her. One lady who read her story tracked Resa down at work. She really needed to talk to her.

They had lunch together when Resa discovered her new friend had 180 pounds to lose. Meeting and talking with her brought back so many memories of her own ordeal. Resa ended up in tears! "She said I inspired her," Resa told me. "I hope I can encourage her to lose the weight, it would mean so much to me!"

That's what it's all about! I hear all the time, "Richard, you're such an inspiration." That's great and I truly thank everyone who feels that way about me! But I want you to take a look around. There're a million other "Richard Simmonses" out there to inspire you, one of their names is Resa!

NOW YOU SEE HIM ...

Michael's Story

*M*ichael wanted to commit suicide. At his lowest point but trying to maintain a little hope, he wrote me. "I think you are my last hope and I don't know where to turn. I must weigh close to 1,000 pounds. I'm doing a life sentence locked inside a body of fat. I struggle an hour in the morning just getting out of bed so I can go to work and support my family. Every day I wake up on a diet and every night I say tomorrow. Please help me." Michael's letter went on to say he had contemplated suicide for a long time. The big question in his mind was how. Once he decided to jump from a window and end it all that way. He tried for what seemed like hours to lift his leg onto the outside ledge but finally admitted to himself this was not the way to do it.

He tried another route, calling on a friend, he

made up a story about some recent break-ins in the neighborhood. He was able to convince the friend to let him borrow one of his guns.

The next day at work, Michael told his secretary that he needed to be alone to finish up some important business. Michael closed the door to his office, sat down in a chair, loaded the gun and placed the barrel into his mouth.

He had prayed to God on many days to just take his life. Being a devout Roman Catholic, he knew that hell would be his destination once that trigger was pulled. He had already convinced himself that his wife, Madelaine, and son, Mikey, would be better off without him. But sitting there holding the gun, he just couldn't go through with it. Michael was scared, scared to live and scared to die.

Instead of ending his life, Michael decided to give it one more try.

After reading his letter I got in contact with Michael immediately. I told him that too much time had already been lost and that he should get checked into a hospital right away. I thought a complete physical would be a good idea before he attempted to lose even the first pound.

But he rejected my advice. His past experiences with the medical community had been painful and often embarrassing. I wouldn't give up. I made a point of calling him every day, sometimes three or four times a day if I felt he needed to talk. I genuinely intended to drive him so nuts that he would eventually have to give in and thankfully, my plan worked!

I was so relieved. I searched around in his area and finally found a hospital that would take him. You see a lot of hospitals are not set up to handle morbidly obese patients. Now Michael was in the hands of a group of doctors who really cared about him. With their guidance, Michael began losing weight and losing weight *fast!* It was like Hollywood special effects: The Incredible Shrinking Michael. With a one-two punch of cutting back his caloric intake and as much exercise as he could possibly do, Michael dropped some 700 pounds in just 19 months!

On each of my trips to New York, I always took time to visit with Michael and his family. Every time I saw him I had to get used to a different body and face. I've worked with millions of overweight people but I had never seen anyone lose such a large amount of weight and so quickly. I felt his story had to be shared.

Michael and I began doing radio and TV shows together and the response he received opened my eyes to something. Up to this point, most of the letters I'd received were from people asking help in losing anywhere from ten to as much as 300 pounds. After Michael's story began to spread, I was astonished to have letters and phone calls pouring in to me from people literally locked inside their homes because they weighed 600, 700 and over 800 pounds! I came to realize that there is a hidden minority of overweight people shut off from the simplest pleasures of day-to-day life we all take for granted.

Michael began receiving lots of mail and phone calls as well. He had become a weight loss celebrity at home in Brooklyn. His story had touched so many lives that people were now seeking him out for help with their weight problems.

Being the kind of person who would always help out a friend or neighbor, Michael felt he had to do

NEVER GIVE UP

something to lend a hand. He started a weekly support group in his community for people struggling with their weight.

When Michael started the group, he was a real team player. He still had 100 pounds to lose to reach his personal goal. The doctor had him on 1,200 calories a day and the weight was still coming off but more slowly now.

Michael was not too thrilled with the new slower pace of weight loss. He had become used to losing those pounds in a hurry. The one thing he didn't want to do was disappoint all the many people, especially in his support group, who had grown to admire him.

To speed the process up, Michael decided it was time to become his own doctor. He began cutting away bit by bit at the 1,200 calorie plan his physician had prescribed. What no one knew as Michael rapidly approached his weight loss goal was that he was allowing himself just two diet popsicles a day: barely thirty-five calories!

Not surprisingly, Michael's secret weight loss program worked. He called me to say he'd reached that final goal of 198 pounds! I couldn't wait to see him. But when I looked into his face and eyes I knew that something was obviously wrong. Michael looked sickly.

Once I'd begged this wonderful man to see a doctor because he was grossly obese. Now I begged him to go back because he looked downright anorexic. He did not argue with my advice this time.

The doctor was not pleased with what he saw. Michael was given advice that was truly new to him, "gain some weight." The only way to put it is that his drastic dieting regimen had come close to shutting his body down.

The pendulum had swung. Michael started out his life by feeding himself to death and now he was on the verge of death by starvation. Following doctor's orders, Michael began to eat again.

I continued my weekly phone calls to check on his progress. Michael always assured me that everything was going great. He was teaching at the support group meetings, motivating people, he painted a very sunny picture. Sunny but out of focus. I travel to New York often and whenever I tried to see Michael, he was too busy with work or personal matters. It got to the point where he wouldn't even return my phone calls.

The explanation for his strange behavior came in the form of a letter from one of his group members. She wrote, "Michael is in trouble. He's gained a lot of weight back. We are all worried about him, please get in touch, he needs your help!"

How much weight could he have possibly gained, I wondered. When I finally spoke with him that afternoon, Michael kept very quiet. I told him I'd received a letter from someone who was very concerned about him. Getting directly to the point, I asked him, "Michael, how much weight have you put on?"

Speaking very quietly, Michael slowly and unwillingly opened up, "Richard, I've gained back at least two hundred pounds. And worse than that, I've stopped teaching at the meetings. I'm afraid the members won't look up to me anymore. Are you disappointed in me?"

I could only respond that I thought he would know me better than that. I cared about him at 900 pounds and when he was at 198 pounds. And of course he would be important to me at all points in between. I had a trip to New York coming up soon and I suggested that the two of us teach one of his meetings together when I got to town.

I arrived at that meeting a little early and spent some time talking with the several hundred people who had already gathered. Within a few minutes the door to the meeting hall opened and in walked Michael. His fellow members had obviously missed him. He was greeted by applause and cheers as he walked to the front of the room.

After things quieted down, I talked with the group for a few minutes then gladly turned the meeting over to Michael and he spoke.

"I missed you guys. I can't tell you how hard it was to walk through that door. I feel like I've let you down *and* myself, too. I always knew that a lot of people gain some weight back when they lose it but I never thought it would happen to me. I have forgiven myself for losing this round of the fight and I'm asking *you* to forgive me. Please know that as you struggle . . . *I* struggle . . . we will do this together!"

My friend Michael's back to teaching again and he's back to losing weight, *sensibly* this time. He still wants to be an inspiration to others and he *is!* After all, Michael might have gained back 200 pounds—but he *lost* 500! Now he knows that his good health comes first. Now I'm no poet but right here I can't resist:

*The tortoise beat the hare with a slow and
  steady pace,
And that's the same way Michael's going to win
  his race!*

STEP BY STEP

This weight loss business gets me down
it all seems far too hard;
I do so well for weeks on end
then somehow lose my guard.

I judge myself for every slip
and sometimes cannot see
that life could be much better
if I'd be less hard on me.

The truth is that I have lost some weight
and that should give me hope,
but now and then I just flip out
and feel I cannot cope.

I need to look at what I've done,
acknowledge my success
and know there is no hurry
just as long as I progress.

Whenever I lose half a pound
that sure beats gaining one;
if I could look at life this way
I know I'd have more fun.

I need to tell myself each day
to take things meal by meal
and not to get so overwhelmed
by everything I feel.

Exercise, while still a grind
which leaves me stiff and sore
also gives me energy
I've never had before.

So all and all it's worth it
if I can just hang in;
those little steps I take each day
will guarantee I'll win.

BORN AGAIN

Susan's Story

*S*usan was in such a hurry that afternoon, it was the last day of second grade for her daughter, Carrie. She had to pick her up, rush home and change in time to meet a friend for a movie that evening.

She and Carrie made it home with time to spare. While Susan was getting dressed to go out, her friend called and had to cancel their plans for the night. Susan was actually a little relieved. After a long, tiring day, an evening with the family sounded very nice.

After dinner, Susan turned on Carrie's favorite TV show, "Webster," but Carrie didn't seem interested.

She asked if she could go outside and ride her bicycle a little while before it got dark. Susan and her husband, Johnny, had taught Carrie to ride her bike only in the yard and to never venture too close to the highway that ran in front of their house.

While straightening in the living room, Susan was startled by the loud screech of a car hitting its brakes. The sound seemed to come from right in front of her house. She thought, Oh my God . . . Carrie, and rushed outside.

What she saw changed her life. Carrie had been killed instantly by an oncoming car when she rode her bike ever so slightly onto Highway 51. Johnny had to be located and he got home as quickly as he could, but by then Susan was in a state of absolute shock.

As the time went by, she couldn't stop crying or blaming herself for what had happened. There were times when she was alone that she would just sit and stare at pictures of her daughter. She even had thoughts about joining her.

Johnny didn't show a lot of emotion in front of Susan because he was trying so hard to be her source of strength. But when Johnny was away from the house with family or friends, his guard came down and so did his tears.

Johnny and Susan's efforts to have another baby failed, and this added to their depression. A trip to the doctor revealed that Susan could not have any more children. They were not giving up though and started the adoption process through the state's Human Services Department.

To get through these very difficult days, the two of them started seeing a family counselor. Susan's continued grief was so great that she was put on antidepressants. The pills did stop her crying spells but did nothing for the numbness she felt inside.

Susan was fortunate to have many people in her life who had done their very best to comfort and console her. But nothing anyone could do or say changed the way she felt. In the meantime, Susan had found herself a new friend: its name was food.

Food seemed to fill that emotional void. For the next six months, all she did every day was eat, take her pills and sleep. She never really paid attention to the weight she was gaining. Neither Johnny nor anyone else dared say anything for fear of hurting her already fragile state of mind. Susan was becoming more and more isolated from the outside world.

There was one person who refused to stay silent however, Susan's lifelong friend, Penny. She couldn't stand by and just watch as Susan continued to gain weight. She had already reached 220 pounds and was still eating!

Penny had attempted many times to talk to Susan about her weight but was still looking for the diplomatic way to do it. Instead of talking about it head-on, she came up with another plan. Using her artistic skills, Penny cross-stitched a wall hanging with a picture of a sheep and at the bottom of the picture were these words, EWE'S NOT FAT, EWE'S FLUFFY!

When Susan was presented with the gift, she thought it was very cute and thanked Penny. And her friend obviously knew Susan well, because later, when she was alone with the gift, Susan took a long look at the cross-stitch, then an even longer look at herself.

"Just look at you," she said out loud, "this is not you . . . this is *not* Susan!" Penny's gift didn't only wake her up to how large she had become. More important, she realized that she had blindly let herself go; she had given up on Susan. Something had to be done but the question was *how* to lose the weight.

Her dear friend, Penny, wasn't done yet. She had

NEVER GIVE UP

taken the liberty of getting my Deal-A-Meal program hoping that Susan would use it. Well, use it Susan did! She even added her own special system to my plan, she called it, "the swap thing."

Back in the old days when her eating habits were still out of control, it would be nothing for Susan to drink eight or nine cans of cola in one day. By switching to a diet cola instead, she had an automatic savings of over 1,200 calories!

Pulling back gradually instead of all at once, she applied the swap formula to a different favorite food every week. Nonfat milk replaced whole milk, "light" bread replaced regular size slices. There were no more salty chips for a while, she had fresh vegetables in a creamy lo-cal dip instead. Susan was well on her way to recovery!

Today she's a regular knockout at a svelte 115 pounds! After reading her very touching letter of sadness, hope and a new victory, I just had to meet this incredible lady in person.

I visited Susan and Johnny at their home near Memphis. It was hard for me to believe that this outgoing, happy woman had been through so much tragedy and yet had come back so remarkably.

I didn't know that Susan and Johnny had another surprise for me. The state Human Services Department had come through: they would be getting a new baby girl!

These are happier days at this old Tennessee home. Susan says that in her heart, she knows up in heaven, a little angel named Carrie is smiling for her mom, her dad and her new baby sister, Victoria.

As usual, I learned so much from Susan's courageous story. It is easy, sometimes, to use food to give comfort against grief. But friendship, like Penny's, is more of a comfort—a life-giving one.

NEVER GIVE UP

265   RICHARD SIMMONS'

"ODE TO ME"

Linda's Story

ODE TO ME

I walk around in a body the size of two;
It isn't much fun or easy to do.

Everyone says "Why don't you try dieting and
*   running in place?*
It's such a shame, you have a cute face."

But food and I have a war going on,
So far I'm losing and food has won.

I walk in a room and look at a chair,
And I wonder inside "Will my butt fit in there?"
Or should I stand and be as uncomfortable as can be,
'Cause I'm losing this war between food and me.

I go out shopping at the "Beautiful and Big,"
Then I come home and to relax, I eat like a PIG!
I get so frustrated, it's really depressing,
So I say "Pass the lasagna, the turkey, the dressing!"

When I go into the bathroom, I kick the scale away,
I say "Bug off, scale, you're not ruining my day!"
So I go off to work, to shop or to visit.
I think "Why do I want that donut, WHAT IS IT?"
Why can't I stay away from this food that's so yummy,
Does it make me feel good while it swells up my
    tummy?

I'm not going to give up, I'll fight till the end!
Oh please God help me to have just one chin!
There's a thin person inside me, I say under my
    breath,
I just hope I haven't smothered her to death!

So if you see me and think I have no will power to lose,
You better watch out, Buster, it could happen to you!
Those cookies and Snickers are really slick guys,
They'll stop at nothing to cling to your thighs!

So instead of judging someone by their size from afar,
Get to know them and love them for the person they
    are.
You may make a new friend whose love you can
    treasure and keep,
For it really is true, beauty is only skin deep!

RICHARD SIMMONS'

NEVER GIVE UP   268

Hi Richard,

My name is Linda and today is the first day I am on your Deal-A-Meal plan. I have enclosed a copy of a poem I wrote about a month ago. When I wrote it, I thought it would make people laugh but when I showed it to them, they thought it was sad. I was surprised to get that kind of reaction. Even though I wrote it as a joke, the more people that read it had the same reaction. I realized I'd better stop and really look at what I wrote.

I have over 100 pounds to lose and doctors have been telling me to lose weight for years. About four years ago, I lost fifty pounds on one of those liquid diets but I gained it all back, plus another twenty-six pounds.

I would have enclosed a picture but I think I've dodged the camera like a pro for the last few years. If I ever get caught off guard and someone snaps a picture, when I pick them up at the drugstore, I sit in the car and rip up any that I'm in. My two kids get so mad when I destroy the pictures of myself. I'm tired of missing out on life. I know some large people who seem to have so much self-confidence. I always admire them for being so outgoing. I used to be outgoing and loved being around people all the time. Now I find myself pulling back on life. I missed my twenty-five-year class

NEVER GIVE UP

reunion because I didn't want anyone from school to see me like this. I don't go to any of my husband's functions at work because I don't want his co-workers to feel sorry for him because his wife is so big. I wasn't always like this, I don't want to spend the rest of my life hiding behind this fat.

I have a wonderful husband, two fantastic kids and they all love me very much. I want to live as long as I can to enjoy them. I hope you enjoy my poem.

Sincerely,
Linda

July 6

Hi Richard,

Today I received a phone call from you. By the end of our conversation, I agreed to get back on Deal-A-Meal and write you in a week to update you. Well, it's been only seven *hours* since we spoke but I had to write you right *now*.

I can't tell you how much your phone call meant. When I hung up the phone, my husband said, "See, he doesn't even know you and he cares more about you than you do!"

He was so right. I've been on every diet imaginable in the last twenty-three years that I had just given up. Your call today made me feel like I am worth it. My weight can't be ignored any longer.

I'm so glad you like my poem. In it I said I knew there was a thin person inside me and I hoped I hadn't smothered her to death. I thought it was funny then but now that I think about it, that's exactly what I've been doing all these years. I've smothered the person who a few years ago loved to talk and laugh with other people and who loved to get involved in "life."

I've become more of a loner now. I've pulled away from people and I've been dropping out of social situations because of my size. My family has suffered because of my behavior. When I think about what I'm doing, it makes me mad because I know behind all this fat there's an interesting and funny person people would like. It's like I'm depriving myself of having any fun or making new friends (not to mention the old friends I've cut off) to punish myself for gaining all this weight. I can't believe I've gained over 100 pounds since my wedding day twenty-two years ago!

Back in high school, if someone had come to me and said, "When you're forty-four-years-old, you're going to weigh two hundred fifty pounds," I would've thought they were crazy! Now I'm every teenage girl's worst nightmare come true! I often wonder what happened to the person I used to be, the one who wouldn't let anything stop her from socializing and having a good time. I

RICHARD SIMMONS'

NEVER GIVE UP

think that's what I miss most about myself. (Look. I'm talking like I've already killed part of me off!)

It's been so long since I've had a normal weight, I've forgotten what it feels like. God knows I haven't tucked a blouse in or worn a belt in years. I miss simple things like that.

After your phone call, I do feel like I want to try again. I just hope that when I do get this weight off, I can make a difference in someone else's life who's struggling with a weight problem. I know this one phone call from you made a big (I hate that word) difference in mine. To be continued next week!

> Love,
> Linda

July 28

Hi Richard,

Well, here it is a little over three weeks later, I didn't want to write unless I had good news. I was really motivated the first few days on your program. But then we went on vacation and I blew it big time!

I've still lost seven pounds in those weeks so I'm really pleased. I had lost eleven but I gained four on vacation. After beating myself up for a couple of days for not having any self-control, I decided to give myself a break and just get back on the program and try harder.

I've really started to take the time and try to figure out what triggers my overeating. I realize now that a lot of it has to do with stress. While we were on vacation, we were traveling on some very busy roads with all kinds of big trucks and other traffic. As soon as we'd stop the car I was shoving something in my mouth. When we got back home, I found myself overwhelmed with the work that piled up on my desk. I felt like if I ate something, I'd feel more relaxed. But instead of eating when I got in from the office, I put your *Stretching to the Classics* tape in and oh boy did it help! Just that fifteen minutes of calm music and stretching worked wonders.

I'm going to close for now, thanks again for giving me that extra push when I need it most. I know I get weak sometimes and I need all the encouragement I can get!

Love,
Linda

July 30

Hi Richard,

I know it's only been two days since my last letter but I watched you on TV today. The things you said really got me excited and kept me going. I think you're part paramedic because I feel like you've breathed

NEVER GIVE UP

new life into me. It feels so good to have such a positive attitude about myself.

At forty-four, I was ready to accept the fact that I'd be fat for the rest of my life. Now I have the feeling that there is hope and the old me can be gotten back. It feels great to have some control over the food instead of letting it control me. Before, if I screwed up on a diet, I'd say "Well, forget it, I'm not worth it." Now I've learned that even though I might have a bad day it's not the end of the world. The words of your Project Me Passport have finally sunk into my brain. Now as I go along I say, "Yes, I really am worth it," or "I really *will* try harder today."

I also realize now that I *am* addicted to food and so is everyone else in my family. There isn't an occasion that comes up that we don't celebrate with a ten-course meal and cake! I've brought my kids up the same way my parents raised me. But now things are going to change! I hope by my being more conscious of what I'm eating and serving, my family will be more aware of how they eat, too.

I've become a positive role model for them and that makes me feel great! This has been a terrific week, thank you again for being there!

Love,
Linda

L.A. STORY

Aaron's Story

*A*aron could see the Gateway Arch away in the distance as TWA Flight 443 took off from his hometown of St. Louis. He entertained mixed emotions as the L-1011 leveled off for the four-hour flight to Los Angeles.

Sure it was tough leaving his mother behind, the woman who had worked so hard to raise him and three other kids after his parents divorced. But Aaron couldn't feel guilty for moving; this was his life and he wanted to make it better.

After graduating from high school, he'd worked at a seafood restaurant, a produce market and a convenience store. But that's not what he wanted from life; the creative side of him yearned to be set free and now the opportunity to attend a fine art school on the West Coast awaited him. He couldn't turn it down.

Aaron arrived in Los Angeles with $2,500 in

his pocket. It was money he had scrimped and saved from frying fish and thumping melons for a living. He'd always been good at saving as well as making money, like the days back at Kirkwood High School when he'd sell bubble gum to the other kids during recess and for a tidy profit!

He enrolled immediately at the American School of Art, and once tuition was paid and his textbooks as well as supplies were purchased, he was almost out of cash. Still, he knew he'd be okay money-wise for a while because school fees included room and board which meant meals in the cafeteria.

Thank goodness he didn't have to worry about the meals part, because Aaron loved to eat. His parents split up when he was thirteen-years-old and by then he already weighed 230 pounds. During his stint working at Long John Silver's restaurant, happiness was always just a piece of fried ocean perch away. The convenience store job didn't help his weighty situation, what with over 1,000 square feet of ice-cream bars, snack chips and a Slurpee machine right next to the cash register. By the time he settled into life in L.A. he was already tipping the scale at 350 pounds!

Oh, life in L.A.! The land of Tom Cruise, endless beaches, high fashion and oh so many tanned, muscular, beautiful bodies. Aaron felt like the uninvited guest who showed up at the wrong party! Always adept at covering his insecurity by substituting humor, he did the best he could to blend into this new environment with as little pain as possible.

The L.A. social scene can be a tad bit on the expensive side and Aaron's funds began to run low quicker than he expected. The money left over from student loans couldn't be stretched far enough to live comfortably so it was time to hit the pavement and find

a job. He knew his fine-tuned sense of humor and outgoing personality were his greatest assets and he would have to count on them to compensate for his physical appearance while he was job hunting. The manager of a local video and record store liked his spirit and Aaron got the job just in time. That Visa card couldn't stand one more cash advance trip to the bank!

He was a solid gold hit at the Wherehouse record store. An expert on the movies, Aaron was perfect in the video rentals department. His store was in one of L.A.'s trendiest neighborhoods and the constant flow of hip, well-dressed, good-looking customers was starting to get to him. I want to look like that, he would think to himself!

Things were going well for him in art school. Aaron's grades were great and he looked forward to the day when he'd get to present his portfolio to potential employers. But when the time came he realized he would also be presenting himself and just what kind of image would that be? He was already angry at himself for not fitting into the Los Angeles mainstream and his self-respect was low. Aaron reached the obvious conclusion; he was going to have to lose weight!

Where to start? Where to start? . . . His inquiring mind wanted to know. Answer . . . the Yellow Pages. Checking the fitness center listings he simply went through the alphabet, not sure exactly what kind of place he was looking for.

Fonda's. Hmm, worth a call, he thought. Aaron called the number, talked to a receptionist who informed him, Jane doesn't actually teach here. "Too busy making movies, I guess. . . . Okay, thank you anyway!"

Undaunted, he continued letting his fingers do the

NEVER GIVE UP

walking. "LaLannes, uh, no . . . Pritikin . . . nah. I'd have to eat too many beans . . . Slimmons? Say, this is Richard Simmons' place." He'd remembered watching me on TV every now and then when he was in sixth grade. "Guess I'll start here and see how it goes." Aaron dialed the club and talked with Teri who insisted that he come on in and take a class that Thursday. "Richard will be teaching then and his classes are just loads of fun!" she told him. Well, if anybody likes having fun, that person is certainly Aaron!

He came to my class and I can recall how he spent the entire hour in the back of the room. Our topic for the evening was stress and what we do to relieve it. Since it was Aaron's first time, I wanted him to feel like he was among old friends. I asked what his remedy for relaxing was and he answered, "Well, I love to paint, it always calms me down and makes me feel better." I thought he had an excellent answer. I have dabbled in the arts myself, it was my major back at Florida State University. I was delighted that the two of us had something in common, besides a love for food!

Part one of our class was over and it was time to start moving those buns. Aaron really gave the workout the best he could but it was obviously a strain. He managed to get through the whole hour. Drenched in sweat and very exhausted, he came up to me after class and said, "I thought I was going to die there for a while but you know what? I loved it! I really feel good!" He was to become a regular fixture at the club.

He started off by coming three days a week, then five days and soon there wasn't a day the club opened that Aaron wouldn't come in. He got on our food program, learning how to redirect his eating rituals.

He never really denied himself the foods he loved, pastas, rice dishes, even a few sweets every now and then. But he had learned the secret of controlling his weight and I can't emphasize this enough, he watched the size of those portions!

He's become one of my weight loss celebrities. After he lost the first 130 pounds, I introduced him to America on ABC-TV's "Home Show." You watched him shrink from 215 pounds in *Sweatin' To The Oldies II* to 165 pounds in *Sweatin' III*.

Aaron is truly one of my favorites. He's a natural with people and I offered him a job on the staff at Slimmons. Anyone walking through our doors with a weight problem can't help but feel some hope after he shares his story, particularly with his own special way of communicating.

Sometimes during class I tell the members about my upcoming travels and what I'll be doing on the road. On some of these trips, I like to work in visits to a local school, talk to the students about nutrition and do an exercise class with them. When Aaron found out I was visiting a school in St. Louis, he asked which one, since he was from the area.

"Let's see, let me look at my schedule . . . oh, it's Kirkwood High School, do you know it?" I asked.

"Do I know it," Aaron shouted, "Are you kidding, I graduated from Kirkwood!"

After breaking into the first chorus of, "It's A Small World After All," I had a brainstorm. Wouldn't it be neat to fly Aaron to St. Louis with me and reintroduce him at his alma mater? He was nervous about my proposition but I told him there was no reason to be. We were going to have a great time!

There were over a thousand students in the assembly hall that afternoon. After I talked and then put them through the first half of an exercise class, we took a break. I was ready to bring out the real star of the day.

"Okay everybody, let's take a breather. I have someone really special I want you to meet. He went to this very school just a few years ago and since he walked the halls here at Kirkwood, he's lost nearly two hundred pounds!"

Aaron walked onto the stage to thunderous applause, the kids loved him! He shared with them what it was like growing up as the "fat kid" in school. He talked about the teasing, the fat jokes, not being able to dress in latest styles like everybody else. He regretted missing out as well as being shut out of so many things.

This was Aaron's moment; he had arrived. If only his former classmates could see him now! A regular fashion plate, he doesn't have to walk past the window of The Gap and look longingly at clothes he could never wear. The power to change his life was always there, all he had to do was coax it out. It took a lot of guts in the first place to leave home for a far and distant city, chasing a dream he's well on his way to finding.

Aaron has transferred from the first art school after being accepted to the prestigious Parsons School of Design in midtown Los Angeles. Courses are tougher there but his grades are still good. He plans to use his considerable skills as an artist (I've seen his work), along with his writing skills to someday illustrate and write his own series of children's books.

I can't think of a better person for the job and knowing Aaron, he'll reach that goal in his life, too. So what about you? How far do you want to travel in your life? The shortest distance between two points is a straight line. So, stay the course, stay motivated and believe in yourself—just like Aaron!

281   RICHARD SIMMONS'

THE INVITATION
Lorayne's Story

*R*ichard, can I talk to you after class?"
Toni asked. She had been a regular student at my
club for over a year and she was certainly one of
my tiniest. She only weighed about 116 pounds
and she never really came to lose weight. Toni
came for the music, the happiness and the people.

"Sure, I'll talk to you," I told her. "I'll meet you
after class out in the lobby."

Toni is one of my favorite students, one of the
things I like best about her is the way she gets
along with everyone in my class, especially the
overweight people. As I told you she's thin and
always has been. But when someone stands up in
class and announces a weight loss, Toni applauds
and cheers louder than anyone. She loves seeing
people reach their goals. After class Toni and I sat
at a table in the lobby for a little chat.

"I'm worried about my mom, Richard. She's totally stressed out lately. She's been married and divorced four times, she's had five kids and still has my two teenage brothers at home and she's raising them all by herself. She's overworked, under a lot of pressure and I think her coming to class would make her feel a whole lot better."

"Well, have you ever invited her to come to class?" I asked her.

"Sure, Richard, but she always tells me she's just too darn busy. If she's not working at her job she's working at home. I've even kidded her a few times and said I was going to have you call personally and invite her to class but all she does is laugh."

I walked to the desk to get something to write on and then handed a pen and piece of paper to Toni. "Here," I said, "write her name and number down and I'll call her when I get home." I got to the house, said hello to the dogs, changed into some dry clothes and gave Lorayne a jingle. The phone rang only two times and I heard a very cheery, "Hello."

"Lorayne."

"Yes."

"Is this Toni's wonderful, hardworking, adorable mother, Lorayne?"

She cracked up. "It is if she doesn't owe you any money. Who's this?"

"This is her hardworking, adorable exercise teacher, Richard Simmons, and I'm calling to invite you to come take class with us."

"Well boy, it sure sounds like you, Richard. Toni is always gabbing about you. She tells me how much fun she has in your classes but why in the world are you calling me?"

"I hope you don't mind, Lorayne, but Toni talked

to me tonight about you and told me you are going through some rough times right now. So I thought I would call and ask you to come and take a class with me. I think that the exercise would help relieve a lot of the pressures you're under."

Lorayne got serious for a second to tell me, "Now I don't want you to take this personally, Richard, but I absolutely hate exercise. I don't do it and I never will."

"Wait a minute, Lorayne. You're telling me you've never exercised? Didn't you have to take PE in school?"

"Nope," she said. "Honey, I faked terminal PMS. I couldn't stand gym class, I don't like to sweat for one thing, and you couldn't pay me enough money to get into one of those uncomfortable, horrible-looking uniforms they had to wear."

Lorayne got me on that point. I know I had my own list of ready-made excuses to keep myself out of gym class when I was in school. Toni hadn't warned me that her mother was so, well, viciously opposed to exercise, but I wasn't giving up yet.

"Lorayne, after you left school, got married, had kids, exercise never played any kind of role in your life? You never tried it even once?"

"Richard, let me tell you. I'm fifty-years-old and I have not spent one moment of those years doing anything that remotely resembles exercise. Knock on wood, I've always been fortunate and had good health and besides, exercise would take too much of my time and I don't have any time to waste. But sweetheart, thank you for being nice enough to call."

Well I hadn't called to force Lorayne to do something she clearly didn't want to do. I let her know that the doors to my club would always be open to her. She could come anytime she liked but she never showed up. Her daughter, Toni, kept coming to class and I told her about my conversation with her mother. She thanked me for calling but neither of us could force Lorayne to give exercise at least one try.

Thank goodness my invitation to Lorayne to come to class was an open one. A wide open one! Because she did finally take me up on my offer, two years later.

"Richard," Toni shouted as she walked up to me before class, "you gotta come out to the lobby! There's someone I want you to meet." Toni grabbed me by the arm and almost dragged me out of the workout room back into the lobby. Standing at the desk signing in was a lady wearing a little white T-shirt, black leggings and a pair of canvas deck shoes. She looked up as she finished signing her name and saw Toni coming over with me in tow.

"Richard, guess who this is?" Toni asked.

I looked the attractive fifty-ish woman over and could only reach one conclusion—"No . . . don't tell me," I said. "This can't be Mom, can it?"

Lorayne raised her arms and said, "Richard, you're as smart as you are cute . . . excuse my appearance, but this is all I have to work out with. There ain't a lot of spandex in my closet."

I told Lorayne she could wear a house robe and curlers in her hair if she wanted to. I was just so glad she came. But I had to ask, "Lorayne, what changed your mind about coming? You told me you hated exercise and you would positively never try it."

"There're a lot of reasons, Richard, but the big reason is the good health I told you I always had, well, it's not quite as good lately. I gave up smoking awhile back because I got bronchitis. I would take a breath and it was like breathing fire so I just quit after thirty-seven years. I started eating, gained fifteen pounds and I just don't have the energy I used to have. For the first time in my life I'm worried about my health so I'm ready to give this exercise thing a try. I know I must be your oldest first timer so I hope you and Toni are right about how this will help."

"Well, you won't find out until you get in that room," I said. Lorayne came inside the workout room for her first class. She watched as everyone else in class walked confidently to their places. Some of them had already done stretching exercises to warm up. My goodness, she thought. How does that lady get her leg all the way up to her head? I'd be afraid of pulling something.

"Excuse me," Lorayne said to the lady standing next to her. "I hope this isn't a stupid question but this is my first time here. I have no idea what I'm supposed to do."

"Go right up to the front of the class where you can keep a close eye on Richard," she was told. "Just try and do what he does."

Lorayne thanked the lady for her help. "I hope that it's as easy as it sounds," she said. Well, it wasn't easy at all for Lorayne. She missed a lot of steps. She went left when she should have gone right, backward when everyone else went forward, she did keep an eye on me but the other eye was on the clock. Man, oh man, she thought, we're only halfway through this thing . . . this is going to kill me. But Lorayne didn't stop. She wanted to prove to herself that she could make it through the whole class and after a full hour of trying to keep up, I'm proud to say she was still standing and in one piece when we finished.

"Well, how was it?" I asked her after class.

NEVER GIVE UP

"Oh, my God," she said. "For a while there I didn't think I was going to make it. I was so exhausted I think I was too tired to even pass out."

"But you didn't," I told Lorayne. "So you missed a step or two but you should be very proud of yourself. I think you were smashing."

"You know what the scary part for me is, Richard? This should not have been as hard for me as it was. I mean, sure, I'm fifty-two-years-old but I should have been keeping up much better than that."

"Don't worry, Lorayne, remember this was your first time ever. Your body is probably in shock, honey. Just keep coming. You'll do better."

When Lorayne got to her car she had to lay a towel on the seat. Her little T-shirt and leggings were soaking wet. So this is what sweating is like, she thought. On the drive home she contemplated the fact that she allowed her body to get so out of shape. She had only gained fifteen pounds but the issue wasn't what her body weighed but the overall condition her body was in. Every muscle, every joint in her body ached for days after that class but Lorayne knew she probably needed more of the same. I think I'll try this three days a week and see what happens, she told herself. It can't hurt . . . well, it could . . . but it'll be a good hurt. Wait a minute. What am I going to wear three times a week? Not that one outfit—and I'm certainly not doing laundry three days a week.

Lorayne went shopping at her favorite department store, Bullocks. She walked past all her favorite departments from cosmetics to evening wear. Lorayne took the escalator up to the second floor to the activewear section.

"Oh, Miss . . . where's your clearance rack?" she asked the sales person. (Well, she wasn't paying full price for clothes just to sweat in.) Lorayne picked out a few outfits and took her selections to the sales counter. "Charge 'em, baby," she told the sales lady.

Toni and I were thrilled to see Lorayne coming to class faithfully three times a week, just like she'd promised herself. She was improving those steps every time she showed up. Lorayne's outfits were always something to look forward to. You know the clearance rack merchandise is always the last to leave the store. There was her bright red ensemble with matching color coordinated headband, the two-piece hot pink outfit complete with hot pink laces in her sneakers and my personal favorite, the one-piece leopard skin unitard. Laugh if you want to, the lady was hot!

Lorayne's body had begun to adapt to her new routine; actually she began to crave *more*. She liked what it was doing for her new body and her soul. And that healthy feeling was returning. She decided three days a week wasn't enough. Lorayne went to four classes a week. She had lost ten pounds already and her dress size went from a 14 to a 10. Lorayne was on a roll, she wasn't intimidated by her classmates performances anymore. She was doing as good or better than anyone else. Hey, pretty good for what she called an "old timer."

Her workouts were going well but not her work. Lorayne had been with the same company for a long time. She had no idea the company was having financial problems. She found out on the same day she got her last paycheck that the company was closing and the entire staff was getting laid off. Lorayne was as shocked as everyone else. But it didn't get her down. Rightfully upset and yes, depressed, she began the tough job hunting process. But before she set out

NEVER GIVE UP

on her daily search, Lorayne started her morning with a brisk one-hour exercise class at the club. It gave her attitude a burst of energy at the top of the day that stayed with her through all those hours of job interviews. She did finally find a new job, unfortunately, it didn't last very long, but Lorayne just refused to give up.

Her new relationship with exercise had liberated everything about her. Lorayne loves to laugh but more than that she loves to make other people laugh, too. Between exercise and looking for a job she actually made time to attend stand-up comedy workshops. She's even appeared at a few popular comedy clubs here in Los Angeles. She bills herself as the "New Age Grandmother . . . the Grandma for the 90s" . . . and yes, she does make jokes about exercise. I've seen her show; she's very funny.

If I ended Lorayne's story by telling you she never found a job but still comes to exercise class, you would probably go . . . "Oh, that's kind of sad." Well, I gotta tell you this: there is nothing sad about Lorayne. She was always the thrifty type so she saved her money while she was working and instead of trying to find a job, she's trying to get straight As in biology, chemistry and anatomy. Lorayne has enrolled in nursing school. At fifty-seven years of age, she is studying to be an RN. She even walks to the university every day, a three-mile round-trip.

Isn't she incredible? For the first fifty-two years of her life she never attempted a bit of exercise. And now she could probably qualify for the Olympic trials. Can you imagine going back to school at an age when some people are thinking about retirement? Instead of worrying about her own health, she's learning to help other people take care of theirs.

You've heard me say a million times, it's never too late to ————————————————————————————
(fill in whatever you like). Lorayne can tell you first-hand no matter what time the clock in your life says, it's never too late for you to try something new, to accept any invitation that comes your way.

I have a very **positive outlook** about "My
Life."

◆

I am **doing** it! I am going **all** the way!

◆

I am worth it!

◆

OPEN A NEW DOOR

Michelle's Story

*F*at people don't feel pain, huh, Michelle thought as she sped her car down Parks Street. Well, Denny, we're finally going to find out if you were right about *that!*

Denny was one of Michelle's classmates back in junior high school, he was just one of many who made Michelle the butt of their jokes back then. Whenever he saw Michelle coming down the hallway, he would shove her up against the radiators.

"Stop picking on me, Denny . . . leave me alone," she would yell at him.

"What's the problem, Michelle," he would reply, "It doesn't hurt, you've got all that fat protecting you, fat people don't feel pain!"

Oh, but they do. Michelle's pain was bad enough *before* Denny became her nemesis. She was always overweight and that kept her from doing a lot of things in school, including making friends. She stayed out of school activities and stayed away from her classmates, never saying any more than she absolutely had to.

Michelle remembered Denny and her gloomy school days as she continued speeding down Parks Street. Her life after graduation was not much different, she got a job at a jewelry company in her hometown. There she sat in a back room all by herself putting bracelets and necklaces together.

It was a job no one else would have wanted but it was perfect for Michelle. All day, five days a week, 8:00 to 4:30, she pieced together the different jewelry creations her company manufactured. She never took a break for lunch with her co-workers; Michelle did not like to eat in front of others. But she definitely liked to eat.

When she got in from work, she went directly to the kitchen to see what her mother had made for dinner. Michelle prepared a plate for herself, took it to her room, and locked the door. Even on special occasions like Thanksgiving and Christmas Day, when the rest of the family sat down at the table to enjoy the holiday feast, she still would not join them.

"Michelle," her mother would call to her, "come out and eat with the rest of us, honey. The whole family is here."

But Michelle wouldn't budge. They could ask her, "Michelle let's go shopping . . . Michelle, we're going down to the beach . . . Michelle, come on . . . go out with us." But Michelle had convinced herself that no one liked her because she was fat.

Of course, that was not the case, she had created those feelings herself, she had become her own nemesis by this time. She didn't need Denny to shove her against the radiator anymore . . . *she* could do it.

Her parents didn't talk about her size that much, they would just give her these "little looks." And when they did make even the slightest hint, Michelle would ignore them, look away and just dig her heels in deeper and eat even more!

Michelle continued driving, she knew that sharp curve in Parks Street very well, she'd driven this road hundreds of times. It would all be over soon, all the pain, the sadness—in an instant she would end her suffering.

Oh, Michelle had tried to lose weight many times in the past with as many successes as failures. There was always a new diet to try and she tried them all. She even flirted with purging food from her body by abusing laxatives, but they only made her sick. Then there was that last diet; she'd lost forty pounds, people were beginning to notice but she gave up again and had gained thirty of them back. She weighed 250 pounds now and people had begun to make those other comments, "Michelle, you were doing so well there for a while but aren't you putting that weight back on?"

"That was my last diet forever," she said out loud, "I'm tired of trying to please everybody and losing weight. . . . I'm sick of it all and I'm sick of them! After today, they won't have to worry themselves over me ever again!"

The radio was on in Michelle's car but with all the thoughts zipping around in her head, it had been little more than background noise until . . .

"Hey everybody, thanks for tuning in to the 'Jones and Jones Show.' Hey, I hope you're not eating anything fattening right now at home or in your car

295   RICHARD SIMMONS'

NEVER GIVE UP

because our special guest today is none other than Richard Simmons . . . Good morning, Richard!"

"Gooood morning," I shouted into the microphone. "Good morning, Boston! I hope everybody listening had a good, healthy breakfast this morning!"

Richard Simmons, Michelle thought, What is he doing in town?

"So, Richard, what brings you to our fair city this weekend?" my host asked.

"Well, I'm going to be at the Emerald Square Mall tonight with good news and a good time for everybody in the Boston area."

"Oh yeah, so what's the good news?" one of the Joneses asked.

"The good news is if you've got some weight to lose and it's got you feeling down . . . well come see me tonight at Emerald Square and we're all going to lift you up. You don't have to be fat, you don't have to be sad . . . no matter how many times you've tried to lose weight . . . I'm telling you it's never too late to try again."

Michelle eased off the gas. Her car was hurtling around the curve on Parks Street and her target was in sight: the tree that bordered the road at the end of the curve. But Michelle didn't slam her car into the tree as she had planned for days. My words echoed in her brain: "It's never too late to try again."

"It's not?" she asked herself. "But I've screwed it up so many times before," she said to me and the radio.

"I want you all to make plans to come out tonight," I said. "Don't do something stupid and keep eating away at your health, do something positive and join us tonight at Emerald Square! I promise you won't be sorry!"

By now, Michelle had slowed down to a sensible speed. What the heck, she thought, I can at least go out and see if there's any hope at all left for me.

Michelle came to the mall that night and watched as we all sweated, laughed and had a really fun evening. She stood way in the back but was close enough to see other women and men her size, many of them larger than her. Funny to her, *they* didn't seem depressed. I bet they weren't trying to drive their cars into a tree this morning. Michelle was almost ashamed of herself for having tried to end her life. If all these other people can feel this good about themselves, then *I* should be able to, she thought. When she got home, Michelle called her sister, Jean Marie. "Hi, Jean . . . it's Michelle . . . do you still have that Richard Simmons Deal-A-Meal program you bought awhile ago?"

"Well yeah," Jean Marie replied curiously, "Why?"

"Because I want to use it," Michele said.

That was all Jean needed to hear. "You can have it whenever you want. I'll get another one for myself later!"

Michelle got on the scale one more time before she started my program. Two-hundred and fifty pounds, she thought, Gosh, I have so far to go . . . it'll take forever.

But Michelle decided not to look at her mission in such long-range terms, instead she would set goals of ten pounds at a time. Every time she lost ten, she'd set a new goal of ten more. She knew she had a lifetime of bad eating habits to change. She couldn't buy that bag full of mini Milky Way bars anymore.

NEVER GIVE UP

She would have to end those "pit stops" at the burger places for a large bag of fries to eat on the way home, too.

She started eating breakfast every morning, a little bowl of cereal, maybe a banana, some yogurt at lunchtime and fresh vegetables for snacks when she got home, instead of a large bag of Doritos.

Ten pounds at a time, Michelle was moving toward her goal. After she'd lost the first fifty, people at work started to notice and their compliments helped keep her going. She was actually beginning to talk with other employees before she went to her job in the back room.

When her boss, Donald, called Michelle into his office, she thought, Uh-oh, am I in trouble? She walked nervously into his office, not knowing what to expect.

"Have a seat, Michelle," Donald told her, "I want to talk with you about something. You've worked for this company for thirteen years now and you've always done a good job. Your supervisor is taking off for a few months to have her baby and I need someone to fill in for her. I really don't know if you're capable but I'd like to give you a chance to take over her job while she's away. What do you think?"

Oh God, should I take this or not? Michelle thought to herself. Fifty pounds ago her answer would have been an immediate, "No, thank you." But she was doing so well losing weight, something called self-confidence was replacing her self-doubt. She had to prove it to herself. It was time to go all the way. "I'll take it," Michelle told Donald. "Yes . . . I'll take the job."

Talk about transitions, her new job meant that Michelle wouldn't be banished to solitary in the back room anymore. Now she was a supervisor with three people in her supervision. It meant she had to talk, to mingle, and actually get to know the people she worked with.

As she lost more weight, one of her co-workers told her, "Michelle, I'll be honest, I used to be afraid to approach you about anything—you used to look so mean all the time that I would just leave you alone. But you have a completely different personality now."

But the real news was not that Michelle had a "new" personality, for the first time, Michelle realized she actually *had* a personality. *She* had been the one afraid to approach anyone, afraid to venture outside her own world for fear of being laughed at, ridiculed or pushed into a radiator. She greeted people with "Good morning, how are you?" or just a simple, "Hi!" Michelle could talk to anyone now!

Michelle kept right on losing weight, ten pounds times thirteen, plus two, equals 132 pounds. Michelle had reached her goal! To celebrate and share her achievement and her new life she sent me a letter and a pair of photos. The photos were framed and matted side by side, Michelle at 250 pounds and Michelle at 118 pounds. You could see the physical difference but you could see a mental difference in her latest photo: she looked so happy.

I called her right away and we discussed the changes the weight loss had made in her.

"Richard, I like myself now, it's unbelievable how much better I feel every day going into work or anywhere else for that matter. I used to stay indoors so much that I would be embarrassed to just walk to our mailbox. Now I take walks around the neighborhood

NEVER GIVE UP

and I've actually become friends with some of my neighbors."

"What do the people at home think about you now?" I asked.

"None of them can believe it," she said. "Donald has been my boss for fifteen years and he still can't believe I've done this. My dress size was twenty-four and a half when I started working for him and today I can wear a five or a seven!"

"You must love to go shopping now," I said. I could picture her trying on every dress at Jordan Marsh!

"You know what else I do, Richard? I get up every morning, have my breakfast and ride my bicycle five miles to work and sometimes I go for walks on my lunch break. And my old supervisor decided to stay home with the baby so I get to hold on to my supervisor's job, too. I've just changed so much, it's like a dream."

"Good for you, Michelle, I'll bet your mom and dad are thrilled for you, huh?"

"Richard, Mom, Dad, my sisters . . . all of them, they say it's like gaining a daughter and a sister they never had. They are very proud of me, we act more like a family now."

And I was proud of Michelle, too. She spent her adult life locked away in two rooms—one at home and one at work. But I tell you when she finally decided to open those doors for herself, well, I just hope *doors* don't feel pain because she knocked them right off the hinges! Welcome to your new world, Michelle . . . we're glad you're here.

BLOCK PARTY
Elizabeth's Story

*D*id you ever meet someone so special that you just can't keep them off your mind? Elizabeth was that kind of person for me. We "met" through the mail at first. She wrote me that she was fourteen-years-old, weighed over 400 pounds and she just couldn't lose weight.

Almost all the kids I hear from at her age have one common experience: being picked on by the other kids at school. But Elizabeth had gained so much weight, she had to stop going to school. Some of the other students mistreated her so badly that she had to drop out of school and be tutored at home.

The first time we spoke on the phone, she had that I'm-ready-to-give-up voice I know all too well. Every diet she'd tried had failed, she would end up giving into temptation every time, she just couldn't stay on any program. Elizabeth was so desperate to lose weight that she even took a whole bottle of diet pills once, hoping the effects would last long enough to curtail her appetite for weeks at a time. The pills didn't do that but they did put her in the hospital.

She comes from a very close-knit family, and they all share a passion for eating. Her mom was overweight, her grandmother, her uncles; they all enjoyed a good hearty meal. Often at her grandmother's house they sat around and talked about all sorts of things. The family's favorite gathering place was the kitchen table, the conversation just flowed so much better there and so did the snacks. If one member of the family had a treat everyone had a treat, including Elizabeth. After they had talked, laughed and snacked all afternoon, then it would be time for supper.

I asked Elizabeth if being from a family of big eaters made it harder for her to lose weight.

"I can't really say that, Richard," she told me. "I really have to blame myself . . . I just get so *tempted* by food, that's why it's so hard for me to stay on a diet."

"I know, Elizabeth, food is very powerful over a lot of us but you have *got* to take power over the food. Your life is at stake here, you're only fourteen years old, if you keep eating this way, imagine yourself at twenty or thirty."

"But Richard, what can I do, I've tried everything, what else can I do?"

"You can try even harder, Elizabeth, and I'm going to help you." I sent her one of my food programs and exercise tapes; that would be my first step. My second step was to make sure we talked every week to make sure she resisted the always present temptation to cheat. She sounded much better the next time I called and the next. But after two weeks, she was off the program and I wanted to know why.

"It's just so hard, Richard. It's just so hard," she told me, "I know you can't call me every day but that's almost what I need . . . someone I can talk to every day!"

Well, I had an idea. "Don't you know other kids your age who have to lose weight?" I asked.

"Sure," she said, "I know quite a few."

"Why don't you think about calling them all up, see if they'll join you in losing weight and you all can do it as a group. I think it would be a lot easier for you that way and good for everybody in the group."

"You know what, Richard, that's not a bad idea. I *could* try that."

"Good," I told her, "and you let me know if I can help out in any way!"

Elizabeth went to her grandma's house that evening to bounce the idea around with the rest of the family around the kitchen table. Grandma loved the idea, "We could fix up the old garage out back," she said. "We're not using it for anything, you and your friends could have meetings out there."

So Elizabeth started making phone calls to every friend she knew with a weight problem. Most of them loved the idea! Her uncle Dave, always a whiz with a hammer and a saw, got to work on the old garage. He put in a new floor, new ceiling, fixed the leaky room and put on a fresh coat of paint.

The garage was ready for her first meeting and twelve people showed up for the first one. They talked about weight and wrote ideas down on how to take their minds off food. Elizabeth was getting stronger. She was "meeting instead of eating." As the

303   RICHARD SIMMONS'

NEVER GIVE UP

group's leader, she would call her members every day, ask "How're you doing today, are you having problems? You are? Let's talk about them." Elizabeth was losing weight too, she had lost over forty pounds and was making new friends at the same time!

Things were going great, until school started back. A lot of the members in her club had after school activities like band, driver's ed or just good old homework, making it impossible for them to meet. Elizabeth got depressed as her new "family" began to fall apart and as it did, so did her food program.

I found out about the group's breaking up on one of my usual follow-up phone calls. The chipper, upbeat Elizabeth didn't answer the phone—it was the I-failed-again Elizabeth I heard.

"Everything was going so good, Richard, then school started back and everybody started going their separate ways. Plus my mom's been real sick, it's just been a sad time for me. I didn't know anything else to do but eat."

"Is your mom okay now?" I asked her.

"Oh yeah, she's much better."

"Well, *there's* some good news!" I said. "But you can make some *more* good news, Elizabeth. Don't give up on those meetings, keep trying! I know some of those kids can still come, even if it's just two or three of you . . . Hey! I've got *another* idea!"

"You do," she said, "What's that?"

"Do you think it would help if I were to come to Portsmouth and teach a class for all of you? Maybe that would motivate everyone to keep coming!"

"Wow, Richard . . . you would do that? Portsmouth is so small . . . you'd come all the way here just for me?"

"You bet I would!" I said. "I can't tell you when

right now, I'll have to check my schedule . . . but I *promise* I'll come to visit you all. We'll have a lot of fun!"

Elizabeth couldn't believe the news when she got off the phone. She didn't even hang it up, as a matter of fact, she began calling her friends immediately.

"Richard Simmons in Portsmouth . . . no way!" they would tell her. Well, let them all be doubters, I made my friend a promise and I meant what I'd said. When I found a "hole" in my schedule, I called Elizabeth up to let her know when I would be coming to her hometown. Now that she had an actual date, she couldn't wait to call everyone up to announce the news with a little bit of "I told you so" in her voice.

Elizabeth didn't have the corner on excitement. I was *also* looking forward to my visit. One of the biggest thrills of doing what I do is not just meeting my long-distance friends in a mall or on a TV show. My biggest thrill has to be actually getting to visit and meet them in their homes. I got on board that USAir jet and flew into Columbus, Ohio, where I spent the night. I got up early on Wednesday morning to start my two-hour drive to Portsmouth.

I've heard they grow a lot of corn in Ohio and I know firsthand now that's a fact! Highway 23 from Columbus to Portsmouth was bordered mile after mile with rows of cornfields as far as my eyes could see. Every now and then you'd pass little makeshift produce stands displaying fresh corn, tomatoes and other vegetables. I wanted to stop, jump out of the car and yell, "Hey everybody . . . let's make a salad!"

Elizabeth's mom gave great directions. I went over the railroad bridge like she said, hung a left at Long John Silver's, drove a few more blocks and there was Grandma's two-story house and about twelve people

NEVER GIVE UP

standing outside wearing black T-shirts that read THINK THIN WITH RICHARD. Most of Elizabeth's family was there, too.

"Hi everybody," I said. "Hi, Elizabeth!"

"Oh Richard, I can't believe you're actually here," she said.

"Honey, believe it, and look how good you look!" And she did, Elizabeth had on her THINK THIN T-shirt, pink pants and black sneakers, I could see she had lost weight, too, . . . fifty-six pounds! "Let's go inside and just talk before we start our meeting," I told them.

Everyone filed inside and we all sat down to talk at, where else, the kitchen table! There was fresh fruit on the table to snack on, no fattening treats this time. As we all got acquainted, they had me signing T-shirts, sneakers, pictures, everything—even paper plates. One of her uncles had a video camera and was recording everything.

"Hey, where's the clubhouse, Elizabeth," I shouted, "Take me to see the clubhouse!"

"Before we go out, this guy from the radio station wants to interview you first," she said.

"Radio station? Interview? How'd he know I was even going to be here?"

"It's a small town, Richard . . . news travels fast," Elizabeth told me.

I talked to my interviewer from Portsmouth's local country music station. I don't know how much information he got from me, I was still signing stuff, posing for pictures and a few more neighbors had drifted over, too. When the radio station DJ was done with me, I said, "*Now* can we see the clubhouse?"

"Oh, one more question, Richard," the DJ asked.

"If I call my wife and she comes over, will you say hello to her?"

"Well, of course," I said, "Now, let's go see that clubhouse."

It was beautiful inside. And there was a man on a ladder putting the finishing touches on a huge mural. His name was Chad.

"Hi Richard," he said.

"Wow, did you paint this?" I asked.

"Yeah, do you like it?"

"Oh, yes, you are *very* talented."

Chad had painted a picture of Elizabeth and I standing next to each other with both of us holding balloons. And there were members of her family painted off to the side looking on. He had painted our pictures against a baby blue sky with fluffy white clouds. A few birds were painted in the background and peppered the sky. Chad was a regular Michelangelo. They also put a TV in the room so they could exercise together with my tapes.

"We wanted it to be a special and happy place," Elizabeth told me.

"And it certainly is," I said. "You all have done a great job in here. Let's go back to the house and see if everyone's ready to get started."

When we walked to Grandma's, I noticed a few more people had gathered and I said hello to everyone as we walked inside. We all sat for a few more minutes in the living room. Every place to sit in the room was taken, sofas, chairs, ottomans, everything. I noticed as we talked that it was getting harder and harder to hear. It was a hot summer day so we all had the windows open. You could hear even more people gathering outside and it was getting fairly noisy.

NEVER GIVE UP

"Okay everybody," I said loud enough to get everyone's attention, "playtime is over, let's go exercise!"

Well, we walked outside and you wouldn't believe the sight awaiting us. There were hundreds, and I do mean *hundreds*, of people gathered outside Grandma's house! The police were there, they had barricaded the street. TV stations were there with cameras. There was a radio station's truck and the *mayor* was even there. I looked at Elizabeth and asked, "What happened?!"

"Hey," she said, "I told you . . . in small towns news travels fast!"

Mayor Franklin T. Gerlach of Portsmouth, Ohio, introduced himself to me and thanked me for visiting Elizabeth and their fair city. He then read an official proclamation: today was "Richard Simmons Day" in the city of Portsmouth! (Thank you, your honor.) He also presented me with a solid brass key to the city. (Thank you very much again.) But then he got to the really good part. Elizabeth was also presented with a proclamation recognizing her working to improve her health and her efforts to help others. The mayor could have named the day for Elizabeth because as far as I was concerned, this really was her party.

Now Elizabeth had told me to expect maybe fifty or sixty people to be in her class that afternoon but official police estimates put the crowd at ten times that, between five and six hundred! Well, since everybody was here, I said I wanted *everybody* to exercise, too. Standing on the street at eye level with the crowd, my view wasn't very good at all to lead a class. But two men brought over a picnic table and tadaah: instant stage! *Now* I could see.

The radio station lent a helping hand and set up

two large speakers. We already had a cassette deck so it was time to begin! What a sight, arms swaying, heads bobbing. Portsmouth is definitely serious about exercise. I played some of my old favorites like "Shout" and "The Wanderer" but I mixed them up with some current stuff, too. For instance, I played a Michael Jackson hit and threw in a couple of country numbers as well. (I like variety in my music!)

Elizabeth was near the front of the crowd and I was so proud, watching her work out with the rest of the people, the people she had helped and even some who had made fun of her. I'm sure she probably made a lot of new friends that day.

We were finally winding down after almost an hour of some major sweating—I tell you it was hot! But before I played the last song, I wanted to say something very important to this wonderful audience. I looked across the crowd and beyond. There were people on their porches, some were just sticking their heads out of windows, and I even spotted a few on their rooftops. I saw overweight women and men, and *too* many overweight children.

"Thank you all for coming out on this very hot day," I said. "You all deserve a big round of applause for working out as hard as you did this afternoon. I see so many people out there who need to lose weight, including a *lot* of kids. You can do this *every day*! And I wish you would. For those of you who don't have a weight problem, I hope you leave here today with a better understanding of overweight people. They deserve your kindness, not your jokes. I also hope that *everyone* leaving here will remember to take better care of yourselves and your families. Your good health is the most important thing you

can have. And I want you all to always be in good health. Now, let's do a cool down!"

I put on one of my favorite songs, Bette Midler's "From a Distance." We choreographed our cool down to the words from the song, raising our hands to God in heaven, then pointing our thumbs to our chest, and then moving our arms in a big circle . . . what a group!

I said good-bye to the people of Portsmouth as they cheered and applauded. Whew, it was quite a class. I wanted to spend a little more time with Elizabeth before I left town but the radio, TV stations and newspaper wanted interviews first, so I obliged them.

After I was done, Elizabeth and I went into the living room to talk alone. A few curious people still stayed around, they were on the porch, looking through the windows but we had enough privacy.

"Well, Elizabeth, I hope my coming out to see you gave you a big enough push to keep you going," I said.

"Richard, I still can't believe you actually did," she told me. "This was like a dream for me."

"Hey, a promise is a promise and I don't break mine. You know, everybody in this town knows who you are now and I'll tell you something else, I bet they all want you to do well, too. They believe in you and I want you to get busy with your meetings again. You're helping all these people now *and* you're helping yourself. That's why you started your group in the first place, right?!"

"Oh, Richard, don't you worry, I'm ready now," Elizabeth told me. "I'm serious. I'm not ever giving up again!"

"There you go, honey, . . . and we both know you can do it. You're going to do a lot of good."

311   RICHARD SIMMONS'

"Richard, before you leave, I want you to walk down the street with me and visit a friend of mine," Elizabeth said. "Her name is Vicki and she's very overweight, she weighs over 600 pounds."

"Don't tell me any more," I told Elizabeth, "let's go!"

Elizabeth and I walked down the street and up the steps to Vicki's house. We knocked on the door and told her who we were and Vicki told us to come in, the door was open. She was sitting on a chair in the living room. Her hair was so pretty, she was wearing it up and she was a beautiful woman.

"Hi, Vicki," I said as I hugged her. "I'm sorry you couldn't come to our party so we brought the party to you." She thanked me for coming over. I began to tell her how we would help her get out of that chair and living again. But Elizabeth took over the conversation telling Vicki:

> "I'll help you too, Vicki. I'll come over every day, we'll exercise together, I'll help you eat the right things. I'm going to help you get started!"

There was nothing more for me to say. Portsmouth, Ohio, has its own "fitness guru." Maybe she could change *her* last name to Simmons. Oh, I'm still checking in with her. The last time I called, she was still all charged up and leading the pack. She doesn't need me to talk to her every day anymore. Heck, she's still too busy watching over everyone else . . . Think Thin . . . with Elizabeth!

THOSE HOLIDAY BLUES

Birthdays, Christmas, St. Valentine's Day
are impossible obstacles stacked in the way
of my weight loss success which I try to maintain,
but Thanksgiving makes it so hard to abstain.

From all of those goodies designed just to tempt,
while knowing the aftereffect is contempt,
for my weakness of willpower brings hurt and despair,
yet those holidays suck me right into their lair.

Halloween, Labor Day, Fourth of July
seem too perfect an excuse to eat cookies and pie;
could I possibly stop my poor stomach from knowing
that holiday lights, food and fireworks are glowing?

Whenever I say ''well a taste wouldn't hurt''
I know for a fact that with danger I flirt,
yet I hear myself saying ''well maybe this once''
knowing that later I'll feel like a dunce.

There's no doubt about it I must be well farmed
if I'm to survive with my weight loss unharmed.
I'm determined to do it, I know how I can,
I'll work out a great indestructible plan.

I'll focus my thoughts on the goal that I've set
and I won't let my mind for a minute forget.
I'll make it a point to know which foods to choose
so I won't have to sing those old holiday blues.

THE SECOND TIME AROUND

Elijah's Story

*L*et's see, Tuesday morning I leave for New York, I'll do three radio shows Wednesday morning and "Late Night With David Letterman" that night. Thursday morning I'll do "Regis and Kathie Lee" before leaving for Orlando to do the Florida Mall on Friday. I have to be back in L.A. on Sunday to tape my latest show then it's off to Nashville on Tuesday to appear at a regional health fair . . . WHEW! And that's just *one week* of my life!

I'll tell you, it's hard enough for me to keep up with me but there is one man working behind the scenes whose sole job is making sure I get from point A to point B, then C, D and E . . . you get the picture! His name is Elijah. You've seen him twist and shout with the gang in Sweatin' II and III so you know Elijah has lost 300 pounds. But I want you to know the story of how he came to work with me and what his life was like in the days when he still weighed nearly 500 pounds.

"Elijah! You get out of that fig tree," his mother, Della, shouted from the window. She'd already watched him devour his usual breakfast, a huge Tupperware bowl filled to the brim with cornflakes, nearly a half cup of sugar and almost a quart of milk.

The rest of the kids in his neighborhood were already out playing softball or hide-and-seek but Elijah had a mission on this hot Mississippi morning. He wasn't going to stop until he'd plucked every ripened fig from the tree in his family's backyard. By then it would be time for lunch.

Just like every other mother with an obese child, Della watched and worried as her son satisfied an appetite that seemed to never get satisfied. She didn't know about the Hershey's bars he hid under his bed to eat late at night when everyone else was asleep. She heard the stories about his walks to school. "Della Ruth," her friends would tell her, "every time I see Elijah walking to school he's got a bag of potato chips or a Coke or something to eat in his hand. I'm sure that arm of his must get plenty of exercise because he's always using it to put something in his mouth!"

Elijah was a smart kid in school, his grades were so good that he was accelerated an extra grade ahead of his other classmates at Eureka Elementary. Eleven years old when he started seventh grade and he was already 165 pounds. He hated seventh grade most of all because of his fourth-period class, PE. All the other boys in gym class always made fun of him, called him names and, of course, they never wanted him on their teams.

His mother actually taught school herself, she loved

teaching kids and has done it all her life. But she was very frustrated with Elijah because although she could teach other people's children to read and write, she couldn't teach her own son to eat right, no matter how hard she tried, and she tried plenty.

Elijah sat in the doctor's office bored and fidgety. When they called his name, he and his mother went into the examination room. "Elijah, how old are you?" the doctor asked.

"Fourteen, sir."

"Uh-huh, and let's check your weight."

Elijah stood nervously on the scale with his mother looking on. The doctor peered over his glasses. "My goodness, two hundred ten pounds, son, you weigh more than I do," the doctor said.

Elijah stared at the floor, embarrassed to make eye contact with the doctor or his mother.

"I want you to take one of these pills before every meal," the doctor told him. "Drop one in a glass of water and wait for it to dissolve, then drink it before you eat your meal, all right? It'll make you feel full so you won't eat as much."

Even at age fourteen, Elijah dreamed of being thin, he was in high school by then and he was so jealous of all the other kids. He would have killed to be able to wear a pair of bell bottoms, they were the fashion rage at the time and everybody had at least one pair.

Wow, Elijah thought, as he dropped his first pill into a glass of water, I'm finally going to be able to wear cool clothes like everybody else! He watched as the huge white pill broke apart in the water and he stirred it around with a spoon to make sure it dissolved completely. He raised the glass to his lips to take that first sip, Yuck, he thought, this is like drinking Alka-Seltzer!

317   RICHARD SIMMONS'

NEVER GIVE UP

Elijah waited a few minutes to see if he was still hungry . . . yep, he was! He used maybe four more of the tablets before deciding they were a complete waste of his time.

There were a number of other tries at losing weight for Elijah. He'd lose twenty or thirty pounds only to give up after a couple weeks and gain it all back. He was the fattest kid at Hattiesburg High and probably the fattest freshman on the University of Southern Mississippi campus.

He was still making good grades in school and he should have, too, because he had no social life to speak of. There were no school dances, no parties and not very many friends except for himself and his sister who also had a weight problem.

They drove to McDonalds together, Burger King, Burger Town, the two of them were true "burger buddies." But as his sister, Kenita, got older and ready to leave home, she decided she'd had enough to eat. She buckled down, counted her calories, jogged daily and lost over sixty pounds.

Elijah was jealous and maybe even a little ashamed. He felt alone now but he simply couldn't control his appetite. Every morning when he got off the city bus on his way to class at the university, he'd get off two blocks before his stop. The bus stopped right next to his favorite bakery and at 8:00 in the morning, the first batch of donuts were coming out of the oven. The aroma knocked you out when you walked in.

"Three glazed donuts and a pint of chocolate milk, please," Elijah told the cashier every morning. In the four-block walk to the campus he'd savor each bite of those still soft, warm donuts followed by a generous gulp of milk. He hated his addiction, he hated his body, he hated himself but Elijah felt helpless to do anything about it. Food had just that much control over him.

Graduation day. Elijah weighed over 300 pounds and it was time to take his degree in communications and find a job. He tried at the local TV station, he tried newspapers and TV stations in the state capitol, Jackson. He tried banks, department stores, anyplace, but he had no success.

I don't understand, he thought, I went to a good school, got good grades, I think I'm pretty bright . . . *why* can't I find a job?

Elijah was smart, but apparently not smart enough to know the real reason he couldn't get hired anywhere: his appearance.

All of his clothes came from big men's catalogues: tan polyester pants, navy blue polyester pants, polyester print shirts and his size 13EEE shoes. First impressions really do matter as much as people say and Elijah's first impressions at job interviews were always his last ones, too.

A full year after leaving college and the best he could do was work part-time as a substitute school teacher and his mother used her pull to help him get that. Thankfully, he still lived at home so his living expenses were low and he could make ends meet on a small salary.

Elijah's luck changed somewhat when he finally landed a job. It wasn't what he wanted, working the graveyard shift at the new 7-Eleven store in his neighborhood. I'll work here just a few months, he thought. I'll save enough money and move to Houston or Atlanta someplace, I'll find myself a better job then.

But Elijah's plans to move were forgotten as he

NEVER GIVE UP

continued working at 7-Eleven. His bosses liked him and put him on the fast track to management and the pay was *good*. He made enough money to buy a new car and help his parents buy a new home. Moving became less and less a priority as he made more and more money.

He was a favorite at the store, got along great with his customers, and who was one of his *best* customers? Elijah! He bought candy bars, sandwiches, cheese Danish and as an employee he had unlimited refills at the soft drink fountain and he wasn't filling his Big Gulp cup with diet Coke, either.

Three years with the company and Elijah was making as much money as he would have at any TV station. He got comfortable and settled but that nagging weight problem was still there. The health problems had started by now, he was twenty-four-years-old and his blood pressure was so high that he had to take twelve pills a day and it was *still* too high. He felt fine though, he was young and the fear of getting sick never bothered him. He had no idea what he weighed anymore. His doctor at Hattiesburg Clinic hadn't weighed him in a long time, the scale in his office only went up to 350.

When Elijah went in to see his doctor to have his blood pressure checked, Dr. Owen was a little bit more glum with him than usual.

"Elijah," he said, shaking his head, "How much bigger are you going to get?"

Elijah laughed nervously as the doctor wrapped the sleeve around his upper arm to check his blood pressure. His head shook again as he began writing some numbers down on his chart.

"How bad is it?" Elijah asked.

"Well, your pressure is up since your last visit,

I'm going to have to increase your medication some more. But before you leave here, I want you to go to the fifth floor, they've got a scale up there that should be able to weigh you, I need to know what you weigh."

Elijah's heart beat sped up as he rode up the elevator. His weight was a "smaller" problem as long as he didn't know what it was, he had simply swept the idea of what he might weigh under the rug. It was easier to "accept" that way. Fifth floor . . . time to get off.

Elijah was escorted by Dr. Owen's nurse past a room full of women and they were all pregnant. They looked puzzled as he walked through the waiting room toward the examination rooms. Elijah was so embarrassed as he wondered what they might have been thinking. The nurse opened the door to a little room where Elijah saw the biggest scale he'd ever seen in his life.

"Okay, Elijah," the nurse said, "Now let's check that weight."

It was like judgement day. Elijah stood on the scale as the nurse kept moving the scale's capacity up in fifty-pound increments, "Well, you're over three fifty," she said, "let's take it up to four hundred."

Elijah figured, "I'll be somewhere between three fifty and four hundred probably." But he was wrong.

"More than four hundred, let's try again," she said.

"Over four hundred," Elijah said, "Are you sure?"

"Oh, I'm sure all right," the nurse told him, moving the balance again, "and that's not all either. I've got to take it up a little more, it's still not moving."

Elijah was in total disbelief. Had he ignored his weight so long that he really gained *that* much weight?

NEVER GIVE UP

"Okay, we've got a number for you, Elijah . . . looks like four hundred eighty-four and a half pounds!"

Elijah drove home in a daze. He wouldn't dare tell anyone what he weighed. He actually hated knowing it himself. But did Elijah feel it was time to lose weight yet? Yes, he felt it was time but the idea of losing that much weight seemed so impossible and the goal so far out of sight, he did nothing, yet.

A few months later, Christmastime, Elijah's favorite time of the year, he *loved* buying presents. He drove to the Cloverleaf Mall with his shopping list in hand. First stop . . . McRae's: a dress for Mom . . . size 12. Sweater for my friend at work . . . size medium . . . size 15 shirt for Daddy.

Elijah's hands were filled with shopping bags as he walked to Waldoffs department store. It was the most upscale specialty store in town, and Elijah had *never* been able to shop there for himself. They didn't carry size 56 slacks! He always looked the other way when entering the store, they had mirrors bordering the display windows and as you walked past them, the mirrors were angled so you got a view of yourself coming, going and a side view as well. Elijah hated those mirrors.

With most of his shopping done, he arrived home to start gift wrapping. Elijah looked at all the fashionable clothes he'd bought for his family and friends and thought about how all his life he could never wear the latest styles or anything even approaching fashion. He glanced over at his open closet door to see the drab assortment of huge pants, shirts and leisure suits hanging there.

He remembered how jealous he would be when his friends would get all dressed up and drive down

to New Orleans for a fun weekend. He would be too ashamed to join them. He thought of all the dreams he had as a kid of living in a big city, of having a job he was proud of and doing exciting and rewarding things. *And* he thought of his last visit to Dr. Owen's office and that scale on the fifth floor and his weight, his 484½pounds. Elijah put down the scissors, put down the gift wrap, pressed his hands to his forehead and he cried.

Elijah cried for the life that was literally getting away from him, and for the life that would never be and he finally realized why: his morbid obesity. He doesn't know where the will came from but something in his brain snapped. Elijah made a vow to himself: Not Monday morning, not tomorrow morning but right now, starting *right now* . . . tonight . . . *I am going to lose this weight!*

That night was the beginning of a new day in Elijah's life. He woke up the next morning feeling different—fresh, ready to prove himself. He limited himself during those first few weeks to about 1,000 calories a day. He had a light breakfast in the morning, a fresh apple and a *very* small bowl of cornflakes. For lunch at 7-Eleven, he'd buy a cup of yogurt and a banana and at dinnertime he'd make a salad, have a bowl of soup, a few crackers and he satisfied his sweet tooth with two cookies for dessert. In the first five weeks, Elijah dropped 110 pounds!

Dr. Owen was amazed at how fast he lost weight, even ran a few tests to make sure he was okay. But Elijah was doing fine, he took a cue from his sister and started running every day. It was tough in the beginning, his first run was actually more of a walk, for about three blocks. But every day he pushed himself a little bit farther and eventually he was running five and six miles a day. The weight was coming off a lot slower now but it was still coming off. In just six months, Elijah had cut his weight in half to 240 pounds. To celebrate, he marched past the windows at Waldoffs but stopped to admire himself in those mirrors. Inside, he bought his very first pair of Calvin Klein Jeans, size 38. They were a little tight but he bought them anyway, he knew he'd have them fitting perfectly soon!

He had fifty pounds left to reach his goal but Elijah was buying new clothes every week. The idea of being able to go into a store and buy off the rack was so foreign to him, he just couldn't get enough of doing it. (Pssst . . . he still can't!)

When he finally reached his goal of 184 pounds, his mother looked at him and said, "Elijah, you need to start eating more, you're looking too skinny!" Those were words he never thought he'd hear, "You're looking too skinny." He had arrived.

Some of his customers at 7-Eleven didn't recognize him, nor did anyone who hadn't seen him in a long time. He looked, acted and felt totally different. He visited his cousins in Detroit every summer on vacation and when he stopped his car in front of their home, they were sitting on the front porch. He walked up the sidewalk as they looked at the "stranger" approaching them. "Hi Debbie, hi Jeff, how're you guys doing?" he said.

His cousins looked at him, at each other and asked, "Who are you?"

"Elijah," he said, "don't you recognize your own cousin?!"

Well, they were so shocked, all they could do was laugh out loud. (Elijah loves playing jokes like that on people.)

325   RICHARD SIMMONS'

NEVER GIVE UP

It was in Detroit that same summer at his cousin's house that Elijah saw a TV show he'd never seen before called "The Richard Simmons Show." He watched me prepare a low calorie recipe in the kitchen. He watched me and the audience during our workout segment and he asked himself: Who is this nut and what kind of show is *this*?

It was back home in Hattiesburg that he got the answer to his question. When my show was picked up in his area, Elijah began to take a closer look at that "crazy guy" he'd seen on TV in Detroit.

He paid closer attention as I talked about good health, nutrition and exercise and he especially loved the success stories. No matter who my weight loss guests were, Elijah could always identify with that person's story. He was no longer watching my show with a slightly sarcastic curiosity, he was watching the show and staying motivated to maintain his own weight loss.

He began scheduling his days off from work only on weekdays so he could watch my show. He was exercising with us, laughing with us and every now and then, a tear welled up in his eye when someone else told their own success story.

When I received a letter from Elijah, he told me, "Richard, I lost 300 pounds before I knew who you were and the first time I saw you on TV, I thought you were just a silly clown. But you do great work and I love watching your show . . . keep it up!" I shook the envelope and asked someone on my show's staff, "Where's the pictures? . . . Didn't he send pictures? I want to see what he looks like!" There was no phone number either, just a return address. So we wrote Elijah back asking him to please send us before and after photos so we could see his transformation.

When his pictures finally arrived, there was no doubt in my mind, I wanted Elijah as a guest on my show. The fact that he'd lost that much weight on his own didn't matter to me. All that mattered was that he'd done it.

Elijah was one of my best guests ever, he was bright, articulate and was he ever funny during our kitchen segment. At the end of each show, you may remember, I always offered a few words of motivation to the audience. Well, for Elijah's show, I wanted to do something different: I wanted Elijah to do it! My producers Nora and Ginger were a little nervous, "Richard, we've never done this before," they said. But I didn't care, I wanted Elijah to close my show that day.

He was perfect, he sat on the set with me and told the audience, "Richard, I know how tough it is to lose weight. You know I've been addicted to food all my life. But the good news is, it can be done, you can lose the weight. I know that's true because I did it and the rest of America needs to know that *they* can do it, too!" (I *told* Nora and Ginger not to worry.)

Elijah's moment in the spotlight was over. We hugged and he said good-bye to me and my show's staff. On that flight back to Hattiesburg, Elijah couldn't get the experience out of his mind. He felt so special in Los Angeles, he'd had such a good time. The check-out counter at 7-Eleven just didn't feel like where he wanted to be anymore. By now he would have been giving up a secure, good-paying job to try something new but Elijah had L.A. in his blood and he wanted more.

Maybe now was the time to do what he'd tried to do four years earlier, he had a new look, a new streak of confidence and he was young enough to take a

NEVER GIVE UP

major risk. So he did; Elijah gave notice at 7-Eleven to the surprise of his supervisor and his family. He packed his belongings into his red Chrysler and set out to challenge life in Los Angeles.

Elijah spent his first night at a Holiday Inn downtown and walked amid the skyscrapers looking up in amazement. (He always loved tall buildings and to this day, you can show him a photo of any American city's skyline and he can name the city.) "God," he prayed, "I want to make it here, please let me make it here."

On his second day in Los Angeles, Elijah came down to visit us at the studio. We were so inspired by his courage, realizing what he had given up back home. As fate would have it, the day he visited us, the receptionist for our show quit and we were left with no one to take phone calls.

"What are we going to do now? Well, I'm not answering the phones. Well, who's going to do it?" they asked.

"Elijah," I said. "Let's give Elijah the job!"

And he was the best receptionist we ever had, when you called the show, you heard him answer in his slight southern drawl, "Good morning, 'The Richard Simmons Show.' "

Elijah loved his new job and he was an instant friend to all of us. He was happy, excited *and homesick*. He missed his family and friends back home and he missed his hometown of Hattiesburg tucked away in the pine forests of southern Mississippi. It was at a weekly staff meeting and I was out of town when he told everyone of his decision to return home. When I got back to L.A. I heard the news. I confronted him on the steps outside of our office.

"How can you do this now?" I asked. "You just

got here, it's only been five months, on top of that, you're leaving and I have to find out from everybody else?"

"I'm sorry, Richard, but I think I made a mistake," he said. "After I lost all my weight, I thought I could do anything but I really wasn't ready for this move. . . . I want to go home."

"Well, I can't make you stay, Elijah, but I do feel like you're giving up. I didn't think you were a quitter, but I respect your feelings. You do what you feel is best."

The staff threw a big going away party for Elijah and I was again out of town but I left him a present of three new pieces of luggage and a card that read, "When you get back home, pack your bags again because you'll be coming back."

Elijah felt uneasy on the drive back to Mississippi. When he walked into his mother's home, the first thing he told her was, "I won't be here long." He couldn't get his old job back at 7-Eleven because he'd been replaced. Elijah settled for a job at another convenience store/deli where he checked groceries, fried chicken and mopped the floor. With a college degree literally in his back pocket, his new job did nothing for his self-esteem. Slowly but surely something else was happening, he was eating again and the weight was coming back . . . five, then ten pounds at a time!

He was sweeping the parking lot at 5:00 in the morning when a shiny new BMW pulled up. Elijah put the broom down and walked back into the store to help his single customer. When he realized it was one of his classmates from high school, Elijah felt two feet tall. His old schoolmate, Douglas, was nothing but nice to him as he always had been, even in school.

NEVER GIVE UP

But Elijah felt uncomfortable with his friend's apparent success and he was very glad after he'd left the store. Surveying his surroundings, he thought, Richard was right, I *was* a quitter, and I should be doing better than this.

Elijah stayed in touch with his new friends in Los Angeles. He was too ashamed to tell us about his new job; he'd just tell us he was still looking for work. When we decided to do a show about "New Beginnings," I decided we should interview Elijah about his new beginning in Los Angeles. Even though he didn't stay, it took a lot of courage to make that move in the first place and I felt there was still a lesson in his story.

We arranged things to make sure Elijah would be home when I called; he thought Nora, our senior producer was calling to chat with him, but he was unprepared for *my* voice when he answered the phone!

"Richard," he shouted, "you guys set me up!"

"You're absolutely right," I said, "Listen, some people here want to say hi to you."

I had everybody in the studio audience shout at the same time, "Hi Elijah!"

"Hi everybody," he said, "I don't believe you did this to me . . . what's going on?"

"We're taping a show today on 'New Beginnings,' Elijah, and I wanted you to share your story with our audience. You lost all that weight and got a fresh start on life, then you came out here to Los Angeles and started your life all over. So you actually have *two* new beginnings."

"Yeah," he said, "but I gave up, I came back . . . when I should have stuck things out."

But Elijah was missing the point. His story was

about conviction, he gave up a good job, a whole *life* back home and came to L.A. with nothing but a little money, the clothes on his back and a lot of hope. It was a very brave thing to do and *that's* what I wanted him to share with us.

After we finished the show, I called Elijah up to thank him for being on with us. He told me he wished he had been braver and given Los Angeles more time.

"Well, pack those bags I gave you and come home," I said, "we'll always have a place for you here!"

"Do you mean that, Richard?" he asked.

"Hey, don't be asking stupid questions like that!" I said. "Come home!" Elijah hoped that little red Chrysler would make one more trip across the desert to California—it did. He arrived about thirty pounds heavier but one of his first stops in L.A. was one of my classes at Slimmons. He came every day, got himself back on a sensible food plan and back to his goal weight. I put him on the staff of my show again as one of our "runners." He was responsible for getting props for the show and since he was always a big hit with the audience, he was also our "ambassador," greeting everyone when they arrived. After that job he wrote a newsletter for my health club for a few years before becoming an aide to my personal assistant. Today, ten years after his appearance on my show, Elijah *is* my personal assistant.

If I told you all the responsibilities he has now, well I would have to write another story just for that.

One of the things I admire most about Elijah is that he lost the weight on his own and he's kept it off for over ten years. You should see how mad he gets when he hears all the experts say that most people who lose weight gain it back—he hasn't! And he wants the

331 RICHARD SIMMONS'

world to know that the experts are only as right as you *allow* them to be. I asked him if there was one message he wanted people to get from reading his story and here's what he said:

> The first twenty-four years of my life were spent inside a vacuum. After I lost my weight, I found out how strong I really am, how much potential I had. I'm like you, Richard, when I see another overweight person, especially someone as large as I once was, I want to say it doesn't have to be this way . . . I see you laugh when I know you want to cry . . . I know the hopelessness and the hurt you feel . . . let me talk to you. I also know that when you look at me, you think I've been this size all my life, but I haven't. I'm still *just like you*. Losing weight is very much like a religious experience . . . we are all part of the same congregation so we have to help each other. I may look like Carl Lewis but I'll always be that "fat little kid" from Hattiesburg, Mississippi. I would not change anything about my life, being overweight taught me to be sensitive to others no matter what you look like or where you come from. If I learned nothing else, I learned to appreciate people for who they are and not what they appear to be.

Thanks, Elijah, you make me more proud of you every day! Now get Claire at the travel agency on the phone . . . I've got to be in Kansas City next week!

THE LADY IN BLACK

*T*here wasn't much traffic on the way to the airport that morning. I arrived an hour and fifteen minutes before my flight took off. This gave me plenty of time to go through some of my mail and perhaps sneak a few phone calls in. I went to my gate, found a chair and settled in for the wait. The first letter I read came from a young girl who was very worried about her sixty-seven-year-old grandmother who weighed 250 pounds and suffered with a bad heart. She asked if I could possibly call her grandma because she liked me very much and watched me on TV all the time. I began visually searching for a wall of pay phones so I could get in touch with Vera in North Dakota. I spotted a free telephone, walked over and dialed the number.

In the meantime, I was spotted by some people walking through the airport. I guess that's not a hard thing to do: I was the only one in the terminal wearing a pair of candy-striped shorts. The number clicked in and I was thanked by a sweet voice at AT&T. As the ringing began, a man on my left handed me the phone he was talking on and asked if I could say hello to his wife, Becky.

"Becky, hi! How are you? I can certainly see you pick out your husband's ties." Becky is now laughing on the phone. "Hello . . . hello . . . is there anyone there?" I heard Vera saying on my other phone.

Now here I was having conversations with two women at the same time. "Becky, hold on." I switched ears. "Vera, Vera, how are you feeling? This is Richard Simmons and your granddaughter, Tara, wrote me all about you. Can you hold on for a second, Vera? . . . Thank you." I switched ears again. "Becky, sorry about all this waiting. I'm on the other phone with a lady who has a bad heart. I hope you understand. Well, I'll give you back to your husband, now. Have a healthy day and keep picking out those smashing ties. Bye, honey."

"Vera, thanks for holding, are you still there?" I said.

"Yes, Richard, I'm here. Tara told me she wrote you but I never expected you to call."

For fifteen minutes I talked with Vera and told her to take care of that heart of hers. It was the most important muscle in her body and she couldn't buy a new one at Sears. I suggested some light exercises to strengthen her heart.

I kept talking to Vera and smiling at passengers when a man came over and asked me to sign an autograph for his girlfriend. Vera was talking, I was talking, this man waiting for the autographed picture was talking—well, I didn't mean to be causing a scene but it seemed everybody was having fun. There was an exception, the lady talking on the phone to my immediate right.

She was a woman of about 250 pounds dressed completely in black: black turtleneck, black stretch pants and a baggy black sweatshirt. Her back was to me while all this loud chaos was going on, completely interrupting her phone call. I remember she sharply turned around and gave me "The Twilight Zone" stare. Her eyes said, "I know you are Richard Simmons and I know I'm fat but I don't want your help so don't you start with me." She didn't say a word, her stare seemed to say it all. I finished the autograph and continued my conversation with Vera. Now here I was on the phone with a woman who needed to lose weight and wanted my help and standing three feet away from me was a woman who wanted me to quietly go away. I lowered my voice and wrapped up my conversation to Vera. In a way, I was also talking to the woman whose back was once again facing me.

"Vera, now you take good care of that ticker of yours and you stay in touch. Give Tara a big kiss for me. Bye-bye."

I hung up the phone, went back to my chair and continued reading letters. I just couldn't get the lady in black out of my mind. You see, I used to wear oversize black sweatshirts just like she had on. I would keep pulling and pulling that sweatshirt down, many times hearing a rip as I stretched the fabric to conceal all my pockets of fat. I could still see her on the telephone and thought about waiting until she finished her call and then going over and talking with her. But I just couldn't.

When I started helping people on this crusade of mine, I had one very important rule: be there when

NEVER GIVE UP

someone asks for help—but never walk up to anyone and offer it. When I see someone overweight I want to run up and say, "I know what you are going through. I know the agony. Can I help you? Please let me help you." But I have never done that. There have been occasions in supermarkets, restaurants or just walking down the street that I've been tempted but I always remember my rule.

I mentally hoped the lady on the phone would lose some weight so she could get out of those black sweatshirts forever.

"Flight forty-eight nonstop to Philadelphia is ready for boarding. Those who need special assistance or who are traveling with small children may board at this time. Thank you."

I still had fifteen minutes to read a few more letters. I waited until I heard the final announcement, said good-bye to the people at the counter and burst out in a chorus of "Leaving On A Jet Plane." I greeted the flight attendant and she showed me to my seat. "Here you are, Mr. Simmons, Four-F. I hope you don't mind if I come to talk to you later. I have ten pounds to lose or they're going to ground me until I do; any tips you could offer would be very helpful. I really do love my job, Richard." I told her I'd explain my program whenever she had a few moments to spare. I made myself comfortable getting out letters, a few Flair pens, some photos and my own stationery to begin answering some of my mail. I had four hours and twenty-six minutes of flying time and I knew I could get a lot of letters done.

"Excuse me, but could you show me to Four-D, please?"

I looked up to see the last person in the world I expected to see—yes, the lady in black and where was 4D? Right across the aisle from 4F, my seat. I tried not to look. I acted like I didn't see her and just buried my face in my work. What were the odds that she would be getting on this plane? There were four other planes leaving at the same time. Why this plane? There were over 200 seats on this 767. What were the chances of her sitting in 4D, directly across from me?

I buckled myself in for a, hopefully, not too bumpy flight. As the plane took off, I sneaked a few glances over her way. She was intensely reading a thick novel by Colleen McCullough.

"Oh, Mr. Simmons, some fresh orange juice? I know you don't want these peanuts, so I won't ask." She was wrong. I did want the peanuts. I love peanuts. I could eat twelve bags of those airline peanuts but I simply smiled and drank my good old healthy OJ.

The flight attendant turned to the mystery lady. "May I offer you something to drink?"

"Black coffee, please," she said, not looking up from her book.

"Peanuts?"

"Yes, thank you," she answered.

I wanted to jump up and say, "No, no . . . not the nuts—it's all fat . . . they're greasy . . . don't eat them." But I didn't. *Remember* the rule, Richard, remember the rule.

The lady in black tore the first metallic bag of peanuts open and spread them out on the napkin next to her coffee. Without looking away from the pages, she felt around, grabbed a few and tossed them into her mouth. She opened the second bag and poured them into her cupped hand and ate them like I used

NEVER GIVE UP

to eat peanuts. You know, sort of letting them drop in your mouth, a few at a time.

"In just a few minutes, we'll be coming through the cabin with breakfast. Please put your tray table down." I was so hungry and I don't mind telling you I salivated over the lady in black's peanuts.

"Mr. Simmons, your choices this morning are western omelette with fried potatoes, pancakes with warm pecan maple syrup and sausage or we have a fruit plate and yogurt. I know . . . you want the fruit plate, right . . . silly me."

Oh, I wanted the pancakes, I wanted the sausage, I wanted the omelette filled with peppers, chopped tomato and onion surrounded by fried crispy brown potatoes. But I thought about pulling my black sweatshirt lower until it almost hit the ground. I had the fruit and yogurt.

"Miss, would you like the western omelette with fried potatoes, pancakes with maple syrup and sausage or the fruit plate?"

"I'll have the pancakes and sausage and some more black coffee."

I don't have to tell you what I wanted to do. But I kept quiet and tried extremely hard to focus on my letter writing.

I peeked as she buttered the pancakes and dribbled the syrup, watching as it ran all over those fluffy devils and floated under the sausage patties. I'd had that very same breakfast at least a thousand times as a kid. Thank God memories have no calories!

By this time, my tongue was tied. I had tension in my stomach and I kept looking at my watch to see how slowly time was passing.

"Richard, am I bothering you? Can I talk to you now?" my flight attendant friend asked.

"Of course you can," I answered as I moved some

of my things to make room for my "classroom in the sky." I took out my wallet and cards and started explaining portions, grams of fat, moving the cards, etc. I did the whole demonstration in eyeshot and earshot of the lady in black. A few times, I caught her glancing over for just a second. I felt like I was teaching her indirectly as I tried to help the flight attendant learn to get the weight off and keep her job. I ended by asking for her supervisor's name and address so I could write a nice letter about her.

I worked nonstop through my nonstop flight, writing letters, signing autographs, sending out Project Me Passports. I got a lot done and my hands showed it. There were black felt tip marks all over. (I'm left-handed so I smear a lot.)

I went to the washroom to clean up and remember looking in the mirror and feeling good about not invading the mystery lady's privacy. I know if anyone ever mentioned my weight problem to me, I became defensive, hurt and angry. Thus, the rule I live by.

I went back to my seat and buckled up for landing. I took one more look at her. What was her name? What did she do? Was the weight really bothering her? Was it a mistake that I didn't spend time with her?

"Ladies and Gentlemen, welcome to Philadelphia. Approximate local time is four-thirty. We hope you had a nice flight, we'll be at the gate in a few minutes."

I watched as the lady in black closed her book, took her glasses off and put them back in her purse. The bell signaled it was time to deplane. She was first in the aisle to get off the plane. We never made eye contact. I saw her the last time as I had seen her the first—her back toward me, her tugging on the black sweatshirt.

NEVER GIVE UP

339　　RICHARD SIMMONS'

I began gathering all my stuff together when I came upon a small note written on a napkin between my letters. It said:

Richard,

    I hate this fat. It's very hard to deal with. Thanks for not getting on my case. I think you're a good guy and by the way, I like your legs.

I just broke down and wept. "Mr. Simmons, are you okay? Is something wrong? What happened? . . ." asked the flight attendant.

I had not broken my vow of silence. She had broken hers and I can't tell you how much that note on the napkin meant to me.

I got off the plane and looked around. The lady in black had disappeared in the sea of people. I wanted so much to say hello and to hug her, but she was gone. As I walked through the terminal, I passed a wall of pay phones and thought about talking to Vera and my first confrontation with the mystery lady. Who knows, maybe I'd run into her again and we'll reminisce about our trip to Philadelphia.

On any given day, I run into thousands of people. One day, I may even run into you. I'll smile as we pass each other. It would not be unusual if I broke into song or danced a bit like the fool that I am. But one thing I will never do is break my rule. So if you need some help, grab me and tell me. Stop me and talk to me or write me a note like the lady in black did. I promise I'll listen, I'll help and I'll *never give up* on you.

PROJECT ME
PASSPORT

1. I admit I **love food** and am **addicted** to it.
2. My weight **bothers me** and I know it's **not healthy.**
3. I am overweight for the most part because I **overeat** and **don't exercise enough.**
4. I have **blamed** many people and many things for my fat, but I must admit **I am to blame.** I hold the fork.
5. **I forgive** those who have made fun of me, judged me or put me down because of my weight.
6. **I forgive** myself and **forget** about all the times I tried before.
7. Today I will make **time** for myself. I will eat healthy and I will exercise.
8. I will not **ignore, hide from** or **avoid** food. I will **face** food and not lean on it.